Dictionary of

ENVIRONMENTAL SCIENCE

Dictionary of
ENVIRONMENTAL SCIENCE

Edited by
Er. Haojam Rocky Singh

JNANADA PRAKASHAN (P&D)
in association with
INDIAN INSTITUTE OF ECOLOGY AND ENVIRONMENT
NEW DELHI

Published by :
JNANADA PRAKASHAN (P&D)
4837/2, 24, Ansari Road, Daryaganj
New Delhi-110002
Phone : 011-23272047
Mobile : 9212137080
Email: jnanadabooksdelhi@yahoo.com
Website: www.jnanadabooks.com; text.ind.in

Assisted by :
TEXT BOOK PROMOTION SOCIETY OF INDIA
4837/2, 24, Ansari Road, Daryaganj
New Delhi-110002
Phone : 011-23272047
Mobile : 9212137080

First Edition: 2019

Dictionary of Environmental Science
ISBN: 978-81-7139-472-2

Typesetting by :
Vardhman Computers
New Delhi-110017

Published by Mrs. S. Chowdhary for M/s. Jnanada Prakashan (P&D)
Daryaganj, Ansari Road, New Delhi-110 002 and *printed at* Balaji Offset,
Navin Shahdara, Delhi-110032.

PREFACE

Environment science is the branch of biology that deals with the relations between organisms and their environment. It is the study of the varied interactions between humans and the world around them, living and non-living. As world's population is growing very fast, as technology advances and human needs and wants increase, our impacts on the world become more widespread and severe, despite improvement in some areas.

This dictionary is particularly useful for environmental scientists, ecologists, geologists, hydrologist, water and wastewater engineers and for students pursuing degree in this subject in various universities. Environment is the sum of all external conditions affecting the live, development and survival of an organism. The potential for adverse effects on living organisms associated with pollution of the environment by effluents, emissions, wastes or accidental chemical releases, energy use; or the depletion of natural resources.

The author himself is expert on environment related subjects and he has written extensively on this subject. While compiling this Dictionary on environmental science, he consulted many senior professors, visited many libraries and surf on the internet for the perfect outcome.

With nearly 2000 entries, the book combines a traditional dictionary approach with a modern and up-to-date style of presentation.

Any suggestions for any improvement are welcome.

A

Abandoned Well: A well whose use has been permanently discontinued or which is in a state of such disrepair that it cannot be used for its intended purpose.

Abatement: Reducing the degree or intensity of, or eliminating, pollution.

Abatement Debris: Waste from remediation activities.

Absorbed Dose: In exposure assessment, the amount of a substance that penetrates an exposed organism's absorption barriers (*e.g.* skin, lung tissue, gastrointestinal tract) through physical or biological processes. The term is synonymous with internal dose.

Absorption: The uptake of water, other fluids, or dissolved chemicals by a cell or an organism (as tree roots absorb dissolved nutrients in soil.)

Absorption Barrier: Any of the exchange sites of the body that permit uptake of various substances at different rates (*e.g.* skin, lung tissue, and gastrointestinal-tract wall).

Accident Site: The location of an unexpected occurrence, failure or loss, either at a plant or along a transportation route, resulting in a release of hazardous materials.

Acclimatization: The physiological and behavioral adjustments of an organism to changes in its environment.

Acid: A corrosive solution with a pH less than 7.

Acid Aerosol: Acidic liquid or solid particles small enough to become airborne. High concentrations can irritate the lungs and have been associated with respiratory diseases like asthma.

Acid Deposition: A complex chemical and atmospheric phenomenon that occurs when emissions of sulfur and nitrogen compounds and other substances are transformed by chemical processes in the atmosphere, often far from the original sources, and then deposited on earth in either wet or dry form. The wet forms, popularly called "acid rain," can fall to earth as rain, snow, or fog. The dry forms are acidic gases or particulates.

Acid Mine Drainage: Drainage of water from areas that have been mined for coal or other mineral ores. The water has a low pH because of its contact with sulfur-bearing material and is harmful to aquatic organisms.

Acid Neutralizing Capacity: Measure of ability of a base (*e.g.* water or soil) to resist changes in pH.

Acid Rain: (See: acid deposition.)

Acidic: The condition of water or soil that contains a sufficient amount of acid substances to lower the pH below 7.0.

Action Levels: 1. Regulatory levels recommended by EPA for enforcement by FDA and USDA when pesticide residues occur in food or feed commodities for reasons other than the direct application of the pesticide. As opposed to "tolerances" which are established for residues occurring as a direct result of proper usage, action levels are set for inadvertent residues resulting from previous legal use or accidental contamination. 2. In the Superfund program, the existence of a contaminant concentration in the environment high enough to warrant action or trigger a response under SARA and the National Oil and Hazardous Substances Contingency Plan. The term is also used in other regulatory programs. (See: tolerances.)

Activated Carbon: A highly adsorbent form of carbon used to remove odors and toxic substances from liquid or gaseous emissions. In waste treatment, it is used to remove dissolved organic matter from waste drinking water. It is also used in motor vehicle evaporative control systems.

Activated Sludge: Product that results when primary effluent is mixed with bacteria-laden sludge and then agitated and aerated to promote biological treatment, speeding the breakdown of organic matter in raw sewage undergoing secondary waste treatment.

Activator: A chemical added to a pesticide to increase its activity.

Active Ingredient: In any pesticide product, the component that kills, or otherwise controls, targetpests. Pesticides are regulated primarily on the basis of active ingredients.

Activity Plans: Written procedures in a school's asbestos-management plan that details the steps a Local Education Agency (LEA) will follow in performing the initial and additional cleaning, operation and maintenance-program tasks; periodic surveillance; and re inspection required by the Asbestos Hazard Emergency Response Act (AHERA).

Acute Effect: An adverse effect on any living organism which results in severe symptoms that develop rapidly; symptoms often subside after the exposure stops.

Acute Exposure: A single exposure to a toxic substance which may result in severe biological harm or death. Acute exposures are usually characterized as lasting no longer than a day, as compared to longer, continuing exposure over a period of time.

Acute Toxicity: The ability of a substance to cause severe biological harm or death soon after a single exposure or dose. Also, any poisonous effect resulting from a single short-term exposure to a toxic substance. (See: chronic toxicity, toxicity.)

Adaptation: Changes in an organism's physiological structure or function or habits that allow it to survive in new surroundings.

Add-on Control Device: An air pollution control device such as carbon absorber or incinerator that reduces the pollution in an exhaust gas. The control device usually does not affect the process being controlled and thus is "add-on" technology, as opposed to a scheme to control pollution through altering the basic process itself.

Adequately Wet: Asbestos containing material that is sufficiently mixed or penetrated with liquid to prevent the release of particulates.

Administered Dose: In exposure assessment, the amount of a substance given to a test subject (human or animal) to determine dose-response relationships. Since exposure to chemicals is usually inadvertent, this quantity is often called potential dose.

Administrative Order: A legal document signed by EPA directing an individual, business, or other entity to take corrective action or refrain from an activity. It describes the violations and actions to be taken, and can be enforced in court. Such orders may be issued, for example, as a result of an administrative complaint whereby the respondent is ordered to pay a penalty for violations of a statute.

Administrative Order On Consent: A legal agreement signed by EPA and an individual, business, or other entity through which the violator agrees to pay for correction of violations, take the required corrective or cleanup actions, or refrain from an activity. It describes the actions to be taken, may be subject to a comment period, applies to civil actions, and can be enforced in court.

Administrative Procedures Act: A law that spells out procedures and requirements related to the promulgation of regulations.

Administrative Record: All documents which EPA considered or relied on in selecting the response action at a Superfund site, culminating in the record of decision for remedial action or, an action memorandum for removal actions.

Adsorption: Removal of a pollutant from air or water by collecting the pollutant on the surface of a solid material; *e.g.*, an advanced method of treating waste in which activated carbon removes organic matter from waste-water.

Adulterants: Chemical impurities or substances that by law do not belong in a food, or pesticide.

Adulterated: 1. Any pesticide whose strength or purity falls below the quality stated on its label. 2. A food, feed, or product that contains illegal pesticide residues.

Advanced Treatment: A level of wastewater treatment more stringent than secondary treatment; requires an 85-percent reduction in conventional pollutant concentration or a significant reduction in non-conventional pollutants. Sometimes called tertiary treatment.

Advanced Wastewater Treatment: Any treatment of sewage that goes beyond the secondary or biological water treatment stage and includes the removal of nutrients such as phosphorus and nitrogen and a high percentage of suspended solids. (See primary, secondary treatment.)

Adverse Effects Data: FIFRA requires a pesticide registrant to submit data to EPA on any studies or other information regarding unreasonable adverse effects of a pesticide at any time after its registration.

Advisory: A non-regulatory document that communicates risk information to those who may have to make risk management decisions.

Aerated Lagoon: A holding and/or treatment pond that speeds up the natural process of biological decomposition of organic waste by stimulating the growth and activity of bacteria that degrade organic waste.

Aeration: A process which promotes biological degradation of organic matter in water. The process may be passive (as when waste is exposed to air), or active (as when a mixing or bubbling device introduces the air).

Aeration Tank: A chamber used to inject air into water.

Aerobic: Life or processes that require, or are not destroyed by, the presence of oxygen. (See: anaerobic.)

Aerobic Treatment: Process by which microbes decompose complex organic compounds in the presence of oxygen and use the liberated energy for reproduction and growth. (Such processes include extended aeration, trickling filtration, and rotating biological contactors.)

Aerosol: 1. Small droplets or particles suspended in the atmosphere, typically containing sulfur. They are usually emitted naturally (*e.g.* in volcanic eruptions) and as the result of anthropogenic (human) activities such as burning fossil fuels. 2. The pressurized gas used to propel substances out of a container.

Aerosol: A finely divided material suspended in air or other gaseous environment.

Affected Landfill: Under the Clean Air Act, landfills that meet criteria for capacity, age, and emissions rates set by the EPA. They are required to collect and combust their gas emissions.

Affected Public: 1.The people who live and/or work near a hazardous waste site. 2. The human population adversely impacted following exposure to a toxic pollutant in food, water, air, or soil.

Afterburner: In incinerator technology, a burner located so that the combustion gases are made to pass through its flame in order to remove smoke and odors. It may be attached to or be separated from the incinerator proper.

Age Tank: A tank used to store a chemical solution of known concentration for feed to a chemical feeder. Also called a day tank.

Agent: Any physical, chemical, or biological entity that can be harmful to an organism (synonymous with stressors.)

Agent Orange: A toxic herbicide and defoliant used in the Vietnam conflict, containing 2,4,5-trichlorophen-oxyacetic acid (2,4,5-T) and 2-4 dichlorophenoxyacetic acid (2,4-D) with trace amounts of dioxin.

Agricultural Pollution: Farming wastes, including runoff and leaching of pesticides and fertilizers; erosion and dust from plowing; improper disposal of animal manure and carcasses; crop residues, and debris.

Agricultural Waste: Poultry and livestock manure, and residual materials in liquid or solid form generated from the production and marketing of poultry, livestock or fur-bearing animals; also includes grain, vegetable, and fruit harvest residue.

Agro ecosystem: Land used for crops, pasture, and livestock; the adjacent uncultivated land that supports other vegetation and wildlife; and the associated atmosphere, the underlying soils, groundwater, and drainage networks.

AHERA Designated Person (ADP): A person designated by a Local Education Agency to ensure that the AHERA requirements for asbestos management and abatement are properly implemented.

Air Binding: Situation where air enters the filter media and harms both the filtration and backwash processes.

Air Changes Per Hour (ACH): The movement of a volume of air in a given period of time; if a house has one air change per hour, it means that the air in the house will be replaced in a one-hour period.

Air Cleaning: Indoor-air quality-control strategy to remove various airborne particulates and/or gases from the air. Most common methods are particulate filtration, electrostatic precipitation, and gas sorption.

Air Contaminant: Any particulate matter, gas, or combination thereof, other than water vapor. (See: air pollutant.)

Air Curtain: A method of containing oil spills. Air bubbling through a perforated pipe causes an upward water flow that slows the spread of oil. It can also be used to stop fish from entering polluted water.

Air Exchange Rate: The rate at which outside air replaces indoor air in a given space.

Air Gap: Open vertical gap or empty space that separates drinking water supply to be protected from another water system in a treatment plant or other location. The open gap protects the drinking water from contamination by backflow or back siphon age.

Air Handling Unit: Equipment that includes a fan or blower, heating and/or cooling coils, regulator controls, condensate drain pans, and air filters.

Air Mass: A large volume of air with certain meteorological or polluted characteristics—*e.g.*, a heat inversion or smogginess—while in one location. The characteristics can change as the air mass moves away.

Air Monitoring: (See: monitoring.)

Air/Oil Table: The surface between the vadose zone and ambient oil; the pressure of oil in the porous medium is equal to atmospheric pressure.

Air Padding: Pumping dry air into a container to assist with the withdrawal of liquid or to force a liquefied gas such as chlorine out of the container.

Air Permeability: Permeability of soil with respect to air. Important to the design of soil-gas surveys. Measured in darcys or centimeters-per-second.

Air Plenum: Any space used to convey air in a building, furnace, or structure. The space above a suspended ceiling is often used as an air plenum.

Air Pollutant: Any substance in air that could, in high enough concentration, harm man, other animals, vegetation, or material. Pollutants may include almost any natural or artificial composition of airborne matter capable of being airborne. They may be in the form of solid particles, liquid droplets, gases, or in combination thereof. Generally, they fall into two main groups:

1. those emitted directly from identifiable sources and
2. those produced in the air by interaction between two or more primary pollutants, or by reaction with normal atmospheric constituents, with or without photo activation. Exclusive of pollen, fog, and dust, which are of natural origin, about 100 contaminants have been identified. Air pollutants are often grouped in categories for ease in classification; some of he categories are: solids, sulfur compounds, volatile organic chemicals, particulate matter, nitrogen compounds, oxygen compounds, halogen compounds, radioactive compound, and odors.

Air Pollution: The presence of contaminants or pollutant substances in the air that interfere with human health or welfare, or produce other harmful environmental effects.

Air Pollution Control Device: Mechanism or equipment that cleans emissions generated by a source (*e.g.* an incinerator, industrial smokestack, or an automobile exhaust system) by removing pollutants that would otherwise be released to the atmosphere.

Air Pollution Episode: A period of abnormally high concentration of air pollutants, often due to low winds and temperature inversion, that can cause illness and death. (See: episode, pollution.)

Air Quality Control Region: An interstate or intrastate area designated by the U.S. Environmental Protection Agency (EPA) for the attainment and maintenance of National Ambient Air Quality Standards (NAAQS).

Air Quality Criteria: The levels of pollution and lengths of exposure above which adverse health and welfare effects may occur.

Air Quality Standards: The level of pollutants prescribed by regulations that are not be exceeded during a given time in a defined area.

Air Sparging: Injecting air or oxygen into an aquifer to strip or flush volatile contaminants as air bubbles up through The ground water and is captured by a vapor extraction system.

Air Stripping: A treatment system that removes volatile organic compounds (VOCs) from contaminated ground water or surface water by forcing an airstream through the water and causing the compounds to evaporate.

Air Toxics: Any air pollutant for which a national ambient air quality standard (NAAQS) does not exist (*i.e.* excluding ozone, carbon monoxide, PM-10, sulfur dioxide, nitrogen oxide) that may reasonably be anticipated to cause cancer; respiratory, cardiovascular, or developmental effects; reproductive dysfunctions, neurological disorders, heritable gene mutations, or other serious or irreversible chronic or acute health effects in humans.

Airborne Particulates: Total suspended particulate matter found in the atmosphere as solid particles or liquid droplets. Chemical composition of particulates varies widely, depending on location and time of year. Sources of airborne particulates include: dust, emissions from industrial processes, combustion products from the burning of wood and coal, combustion products associated with motor vehicle or non-road engine exhausts, and reactions to gases in the atmosphere.

Airborne Release: Release of any pollutant into the air.

Alachlor: A herbicide, marketed under the trade name Lasso, used mainly to control weeds in corn and soybean fields.

Alar: Trade name for daminozide, a pesticide that makes apples redder, firmer, and less likely to drop off trees before growers are ready to pick them. It is also used to a lesser extent on peanuts, tart cherries, concord grapes, and other fruits.

Aldicarb: An insecticide sold under the trade name Temik. It is made from ethyl isocyanate.

Algae: Simple rootless plants that grow in sunlit waters in proportion to the amount of available nutrients. They can affect water quality adversely by lowering the dissolved oxygen in the water. They are food for fish and small aquatic animals.

Algal Blooms: Sudden spurts of algal growth, which can affect water quality adversely and indicate potentially hazardous changes in local water chemistry.

Algaecide: Substance or chemical used specifically to kill or control algae.

Aliquot: A measured portion of a sample taken for analysis. One or more aliquots make up a sample.

Alkaline: The condition of water or soil which contains a sufficient amount of alkali substance to raise the pH above 7.0.

Alkalinity: The capacity of bases to neutralize acids. An example is lime added to lakes to decrease acidity.

Allergen: A substance that causes an allergic reaction in individuals sensitive to it.

Alluvial: Relating to and/or sand deposited by flowing water.

Alternate Method: Any method of sampling and analyzing for an air or water pollutant that is not a reference or equivalent method but that has been demonstrated in specific cases-to EPA's satisfaction to produce results adequate for compliance monitoring.

Alternative Compliance: A policy that allows facilities to choose among methods for achieving emission-reduction or risk-reduction instead of command-and control regulations that specify standards and how to meet them. Use of a theoretical emissions bubble over a facility to cap the amount of pollution emitted while allowing the company to choose where and how (within the facility) it complies.(See: bubble, emissions trading.)

Alternative Fuels: Substitutes for traditional liquid, oil-derived motor vehicle fuels like gasoline and diesel. Includes mixtures of alcohol-based fuels with gasoline, methanol, ethanol, compressed natural gas, and others.

Alternative Remedial Contract Strategy Contractors: Government contractors who provide project management and technical services to support remedial response activities at National Priorities List sites.

Ambient Air: Any unconfined portion of the atmosphere: open air, surrounding air.

Ambient Air Quality Standards: (See: Criteria Pollutants and National Ambient Air Quality Standards.)

Ambient Measurement: A measurement of the concentration of a substance or pollutant within the immediate environs of an organism; taken to relate it to the amount of possible exposure.

Ambient Medium: Material surrounding or contacting an organism (*e.g.* outdoor air, indoor air, water, or soil, through which chemicals or pollutants can reach the organism. (See: biological medium, environmental medium.)

Ambient Temperature: Temperature of the surrounding air or other medium.

Amprometric Titration: A way of measuring concentrations of certain substances in water using an electric current that flows during a chemical reaction.

Anaerobic: A life or process that occurs in, or is not destroyed by, the absence of oxygen.

Anaerobic Decomposition: Reduction of the net energy level and change in chemical composition of organic matter caused by microorganisms in an oxygen-free environment.

Animal Dander: Tiny scales of animal skin, a common indoor air pollutant.

Animal Studies: Investigations using animals as surrogates for humans with the expectation that the results are pertinent to humans.

Anisotropy: In hydrology, the conditions under which one or more hydraulic properties of an aquifer vary from a reference point.

Annular Space, Annulus: The space between two concentric tubes or casings, or between the casing and the borehole wall.

Antagonism: Interference or inhibition of the effect of one chemical by the action of another.

Antarctic "Ozone Hole": Refers to the seasonal depletion of ozone in the upper atmosphere above a large area of Antarctica. (See: Ozone Hole.)

Anti-Degradation Clause: Part of federal air quality and water quality requirements prohibiting deterioration where pollution levels are above the legal limit.

Anti-Microbial: An agent that kills microbes.

Applicable or Relevant and Appropriate Requirements (ARARs): Any state or federal statute that pertains to protection of human life and the environment in addressing specific conditions or use of a particular cleanup technology at a Superfund site.

Applied Dose: In exposure assessment, the amount of a substance in contact with the primary absorption boundaries of an organism (*e.g.* skin, lung tissue, gastrointestinal track) and available for absorption.

Aqueous: Something made up of water.

Aqueous Solubility: The maximum concentration of a chemical that will dissolve in pure water at a reference temperature.

Aquifer: An underground geological formation, or group of formations, containing water. Are sources of groundwater for wells and springs.

Aquifer Test: A test to determine hydraulic properties of an aquifer.

Aquitard: Geological formation that may contain groundwater but is not capable of transmitting significant quantities of it under normal hydraulic gradients. May function as confining bed.

Architectural Coatings: Coverings such as paint and roof tar that are used on exteriors of buildings.

Area of Review: In the UIC program, the area surrounding an injection well that is reviewed during the permitting process to determine if flow between aquifers will be induced by the injection operation.

Area Source: Any source of air pollution that is released over a relatively small area but which cannot be classified as a point source. Such sources may include vehicles and other small engines, small businesses and household activities, or biogenic sources such as a forest that releases hydrocarbons.

Aromatics: A type of hydrocarbon, such as benzene or toluene, with a specific type of ring structure. Aromatics are sometimes added to gasoline in order to increase octane. Some aromatics are toxic.

Arsenicals: Pesticides containing arsenic.

Artesian (Aquifer or Well): Water held under pressure in porous rock or soil confined by impermeable geological formations.

Asbestos: A mineral fiber that can pollute air or water and cause cancer or asbestosis when inhaled. EPA has banned or severely restricted its use in manufacturing and construction.

Asbestos Abatement: Procedures to control fiber release from asbestos-containing materials in a building or to remove them entirely, including removal, encapsulation, repair, enclosure, encasement, and operations and maintenance programs.

Asbestos Assessment: In the asbestos-in-schools program, the evaluation of the physical condition and potential for damage of all friable asbestos containing materials and thermal insulation systems.

Asbestos Program Manager: A building owner or designated representative who supervises all aspects of the facility asbestos management and control program.

Asbestos-Containing Waste Materials (ACWM): Mill tailings or any waste that contains commercial asbestos and is generated by a source covered by the Clean Air Act Asbestos NESHAPS.

Asbestosis: A disease associated with inhalation of asbestos fibers. The disease makes breathing progressively more difficult and can be fatal.

Ash: The mineral content of a product remaining after complete combustion.

Assay: A test for a specific chemical, microbe, or effect.

Assessment Endpoint: In ecological risk assessment, an explicit expression of the environmental value to be protected; includes both an ecological entity and specific attributed thereof. entity (*e.g.* salmon are a valued ecological entity; reproduction and population maintenance—the attribute—form an assessment endpoint.)

Assimilation: The ability of a body of water to purify itself of pollutants.

Assimilative Capacity: The capacity of a natural body of water to receive wastewaters or toxic materials without deleterious effects and without damage to aquatic life or humans who consume the water.

Association of Boards of Certification: An international organization representing boards which certify the operators of waterworks and wastewater facilities.

Attainment Area: An area considered to have air quality as good as or better than the national ambient air quality standards as defined in the Clean Air Act. An area may be an attainment area for one pollutant and a non-attainment area for others.

Attenuation: The process by which a compound is reduced in concentration over time, through absorption, adsorption, degradation, dilution, and/or transformation. an also be the decrease with distance of sight caused by attenuation of light by particulate pollution.

Attractant: A chemical or agent that lures insects or other pests by stimulating their sense of smell.

Attrition: Wearing or grinding down of a substance by friction. Dust from such processes contributes to air pollution.

Availability Session: Informal meeting at a public location where interested citizens can talk with EPA and state officials on a one-to-one basis.

Available Chlorine: A measure of the amount of chlorine available in chlorinated lime, hypochlorite compounds, and other materials used as a source of chlorine when compared with that of liquid or gaseous chlorines.

Avoided Cost: The cost a utility would incur to generate the next increment of electric capacity using its own resources; many landfill gas projects' buy back rates are based on avoided costs.

B

Back Pressure: A pressure that can cause water to backflow into the water supply when a user's waste water system is at a higher pressure than the public system.

Backflow/Back Siphonage: A reverse flow condition created by a difference in water pressures that causes water to flow back into the distribution pipes of a drinking water supply from any source other than the intended one.

Background Level: 1. The concentration of a substance in an environmental media (air, water, or soil) that occurs naturally or is not the result of human activities. 2. In exposure assessment the concentration of a substance in a defined control area, during a fixed period of time before, during, or after a data-gathering operation.

Backwashing: Reversing the flow of water back through the filter media to remove entrapped solids.

Backyard Composting: Diversion of organic food waste and yard trimmings from the municipal waste stream by composting hem in one's yard through controlled decomposition of organic matter by bacteria and fungi into a humus-like product. It is considered source reduction, not recycling, because the composted materials never enter the municipal waste stream.

Barrel Sampler: Open-ended steel tube used to collect soil samples.

BACT - Best Available Control Technology: An emission limitation based on the maximum degree of emission reduction (considering energy, environmental, and economic impacts) achievable through application of production processes and available methods, systems, and techniques. BACT does not permit emissions in excess of those allowed under any applicable Clean Air Act provisions. Use of the BACT concept is allowable on a case by case basis for major new or modified emissions sources in attainment areas and applies to each regulated pollutant.

Bacteria: (Singular: bacterium) Microscopic living organisms that can aid in pollution control by metabolizing organic matter in sewage, oil spills or other pollutants. However, bacteria in soil, water or air can also cause human, animal and plant health problems.

Bactericide: A pesticide used to control or destroy bacteria, typically in the home, schools, or hospitals.

Baffle: A flat board or plate, deflector, guide, or similar device constructed or placed in flowing water or slurry systems to cause more uniform flow velocities to absorb energy and to divert, guide, or agitate liquids.

Baffle Chamber: In incinerator design, a chamber designed to promote the settling of fly ash and coarse particulate matter by changing the direction and/or reducing the velocity of the gases produced by the combustion of the refuse or sludge.

Baghouse Filter: Large fabric bag, usually made of glass fibers, used to eliminate intermediate and large (greater than 20 PM in diameter) particles. This device operates like the bag of an electric vacuum cleaner, passing the air and smaller particles while entrapping the larger ones.

Bailer: 1. A pipe with a valve at the lower end, used to remove slurry from the bottom or side of a well as it is being drilled, or to collect groundwater samples from wells or open boreholes. 2. A tube of varying length.

Baling: Compacting solid waste into blocks to reduce volume and simplify handling.

Ballistic Separator: A machine that sorts organic from inorganic matter for composting.

Band Application: The spreading of chemicals over, or next to, each row of plants in a field.

Banking: A system for recording qualified air emission reductions for later use in bubble, offset, or netting transactions. (See: emissions trading.)

Bar Screen: In wastewater treatment, a device used to remove large solids.

Barrier Coating(s): A layer of a material that obstructs or prevents passage of something through a surface that is to be protected; *e.g.*, grout, caulk, or various sealing compounds; sometimes used with polyurethane membranes to prevent corrosion or oxidation of metal surfaces, chemical impacts on various materials, or, for example, to prevent radon infiltration through walls, cracks, or joints in a house.

Basal Application: In pesticides, the application of a chemical on plant stems or tree trunks just above the soil line.

Basalt: Consistent year-round energy use of a facility; also refers to the minimum amount of electricity supplied continually to a facility.

Bean Sheet: Common term for a pesticide data package record.

Bed Load: Sediment particles resting on or near the channel bottom that are pushed or rolled along by the flow of water.

BEN: EPA's computer model for analyzing a violator's economic gain from not complying with the law.

Bench-scale Tests: Laboratory testing of potential cleanup technologies (See: treatability studies.)

Benefit-Cost Analysis: An economic method for assessing the benefits and costs of achieving alternative health-based standards at given levels of health protection.

Benthic/Benthos: An organism that feeds on the sediment at the bottom of a water body such as an ocean, lake, or river.

Bentonite: A colloidal clay, expansible when moist, commonly used to provide a tight seal around a well casing.

Beryllium: An metal hazardous to human health when inhaled as an airborne pollutant. It is discharged by machine shops, ceramic and propellant plants, and foundries.

Best Available Control Measures (BACM): A term used to refer to the most effective measures (according to EPA guidance) for controlling small or dispersed particulates and other emissions from sources such as roadway dust, soot and ash from woodstoves and open burning of rush, timber, grasslands, or trash.

Best Available Control Technology (BACT): For any specific source, the currently available technology producing the greatest reduction of air pollutant emissions,taking into account energy, environmental, economic, and other costs.

Best Demonstrated Available Technology (BDAT): As identified by EPA, the most effective commercially available means of treating specific types of hazardous waste. The BDATs may change with advances in treatment technologies.

Best Management Practice (BMP): Methods that have been determined to be the most effective, practical means of preventing or reducing pollution from non-point sources.

Bimetal: Beverage containers with steel bodies and aluminum tops; handled differently from pure aluminum in recycling.

Bioaccumulants: Substances that increase in concentration in living organisms as they take in contaminated air, water, or food because the substances are very slowly metabolized or excreted. (See: biological magnification.)

Bioassay: A test to determine te relative strength of a substance by comparing its effect on a test organism with that of a standard preparation.

Bioavailabiliity: Degree of ability to be absorbed and ready to interact in organism metabolism.

Biochemical Oxygen Demand (BOD): A measure of the amount of oxygen consumed in the biological processes that break down organic matter in water. The greater the BOD, the greater the degree of pollution.

Bioconcentration: The accumulation of a chemical in tissues of a fish or other organism to levels greater than in the surrounding medium.

Biodegradable: Capable of decomposing under natural conditions.

Biodiversity: Refers to the variety and variability among living organisms and the ecological complexes in which they occur. Diversity can be defined as the number of different items and their relative frequencies. For biological diversity, these items are organized at many levels, ranging from complete ecosystems to the biochemical structures that are the molecular basis of heredity. Thus, the term encompasses different ecosystems, species, and genes.

Biological Contaminants: Living organisms or derivates (*e.g.* viruses, bacteria, fungi, and mammal and bird antigens) that can cause harmful health effects when inhaled, swallowed, or otherwise taken into the body.

Biological Control: In pest control, the use of animals and organisms that eat or otherwise kill or out-compete pests.

Biological Integrity: The ability to support and maintain balanced, integrated, functionality in the natural habitat of a given region. Concept is applied primarily in drinking water management.

Biological Magnification: Refers to the process whereby certain substances such as pesticides or heavy metals move up the food chain, work their way into rivers or lakes, and are eaten by aquatic organisms such as fish, which in turn are eaten by large birds, animals or humans. The substances become concentrated in tissues or internal organs as they move up the chain. (See: bioaccumulants.)

Biological Measurement: A measurement taken in a biological medium. For exposure assessment, it is related to the measurement is taken to related it to the established internal dose of a compound.

Biological Medium: One of the major component of an organism; *e.g.* blood, fatty tissue, lymph nodes or breath, in which chemicals can be stored or transformed. (See: ambient medium, environmental medium.)

Biological Oxidation: Decomposition of complex organic materials by microorganisms. Occurs in self-purification of water bodies and in activated sludge wastewater treatment.

Biological Oxygen Demand (BOD): An indirect measure of the concentration of biologically degradable material present in organic wastes. It usually reflects the amount of oxygen consumed in five days by biological processes breaking down organic waste.

Biological pesticides: Certain microorganism, including bacteria, fungi, viruses, and protozoa that are effective in controlling pests. These agents usually do not have toxic effects on animals and people and do not leave toxic or persistent chemical residues in the environment.

Biological Stressors: Organisms accidentally or intentionally dropped into habitats in which they do not evolve naturally; *e.g.* gypsy moths, Dutch elm disease, certain types of algae, and bacteria.

Biological Treatment: A treatment technology that uses bacteria to consume organic waste.

Biologically Effective Dose: The amount of a deposited or absorbed compound reaching the cells or target sites where adverse effect occur, or where the chemical interacts with a membrane.

Biologicals: Vaccines, cultures and other preparations made from living organisms and their products, intended for use in diagnosing, immunizing, or treating humans or animals, or in related research.

Biomass: All of the living material in a given area; often refers to vegetation.

Biome: Entire community of living organisms in a single major ecological area.

Biomonitoring: 1. The use of living organisms to test the suitability of effluents for discharge into receiving waters and to test the quality of such waters downstream from the discharge. 2. Analysis of blood, urine, tissues, etc. to measure chemical exposure in humans.

Bioremediation: Use of living organisms to clean up oil spills or remove other pollutants from soil, water, or wastewater; use of organisms such as non-harmful insects to remove agricultural pests or counteract diseases of trees, plants, and garden soil.

Biosensor: Analytical device comprising a biological recognition element (*e.g.* enzyme, receptor, DNA, antibody, or microorganism) in intimate contact with an electrochemical, optical, thermal, or acoustic signal transducer that together permit analyses of chemical properties or quantities. Shows potential development in some areas, including environmental monitoring.

Biosphere: The portion of Earth and its atmosphere that can support life.

Biostabilizer: A machine that converts solid waste into compost by grinding and aeration.

Biota: The animal and plant life of a given region.

Biotechnology: Techniques that use living organisms or parts of organisms to produce a variety of products (from medicines to industrial enzymes) to improve plants or animals or to develop microorganisms to remove toxics from bodies of water, or act as pesticides.

Biotic Community: A naturally occurring assemblage of plants and animals that live in the same environment and are mutually sustaining and interdependent. (See: biome.)

Biotransformation: Conversion of a substance into other compounds by organisms; includes biodegredation.

Blackwater: Water that contains animal, human, or food waste.

Blood Products: Any product derived from human blood, including but not limited to blood plasma, platelets, red or white corpuscles, and derived licensed products such as interferon.

Bloom: A proliferation of algae and/or higher aquatic plants in a body of water; often related to pollution, especially when pollutants accelerate growth.

BOD5: The amount of dissolved oxygen consumed in five days by biological processes breaking down organic matter.

Body Burden: The amount of a chemical stored in the body at a given time, especially a potential toxin in the body as the result of exposure.

Bog: A type of wetland that accumulates appreciable peat deposits. Bogs depend primarily on precipitation for their water source, and are usually acidic and rich in plant residue with a conspicuous mat of living green moss.

Boiler: A vessel designed to transfer heat produced by combustion or electric resistance to water. Boilers may provide hot water or steam.

Boom: 1. A floating device used to contain oil on a body of water. 2. A piece of equipment used to apply pesticides from a tractor or truck.

Borehole: Hole made with drilling equipment.

Botanical Pesticide: A pesticide whose active ingredient is a plant-produced chemical such as nicotine or strychnine. Also called a plant-derived pesticide.

Bottle Bill: Proposed or enacted legislation which requires a returnable deposit on beer or soda containers and provides for retail store or other redemption. Such legislation is designed to discourage use of throw-away containers.

Bottom Ash: The non-airborne combustion residue from burning pulverized coal in a boiler; the material which falls to the bottom of the boiler and is removed mechanically; a concentration of noncombustible materials, which may include toxics.

Bottom Land Hardwoods: Forested freshwater wetlands adjacent to rivers in the southeastern United States, especially valuable for wildlife breeding, nesting and habitat.

Bounding Estimate: An estimate of exposure, dose, or risk that is higher than that incurred by the person in the population with the currently highest exposure, dose, or risk. Bounding estimates are useful in developing statements that exposures, doses, or risks are not greater than an estimated value.

Brackish: Mixed fresh and salt water.

Breakpoint Chlorination: Addition of chlorine to water until the chlorine demand has been satisfied.

Breakthrough: A crack or break in a filter bed that allows the passage of floc or particulate matter through a filter; will cause an increase in filter effluent turbidity.

Breathing Zone: Area of air in which an organism inhales.

Brine Mud: Waste material, often associated with well-drilling or mining, composed of mineral salts or other inorganic compounds.

British Thermal Unit: Unit of heat energy equal to the amount of heat required to raise the temperature of one pound of water by one degree Fahrenheit at sea level.

Broadcast Application: The spreading of pesticides over an entire area.

Brownfields: Abandoned, idled, or under used industrial and commercial facilities/sites where expansion or redevelopment is complicated by real or perceived environmental contamination. They can be in urban, suburban, or rural areas. EPA's Brownfields initiative helps communities mitigate potential health risks and restore the economic viability of such areas or properties.

Bubble: A system under which existing emissions sources can propose alternate means to comply with a set of emissions limitations; under the bubble concept, sources can control more than required at one emission point where control costs are relatively low in return for a comparable relaxation of controls at a second emission point where costs are higher.

Bubble Policy: (See: emissions trading.)

Buffer: A solution or liquid whose chemical makeup is such that it minimizes changes in pH when acids or bases are added to it.

Buffer Strips: Strips of grass or other erosion-resisting vegetation between or below cultivated strips or fields.

Building Cooling Load: The hourly amount of heat that must be removed from a building to maintain indoor comfort (measured in British thermal units (Btus).

Building Envelope: The exterior surface of a building's construction—the walls, windows, floors, roof, and floor. Also called building shell.

Building Related Illness: Diagnosable illness whose cause and symptoms can be directly attributed to a specific pollutant source within a building (*e.g.* Legionnaire's disease, hypersensitivity, pneumonitis.) (See: sick building syndrome.)

Bulk Sample: A small portion (usually thumbnail size) of a suspect asbestos-containing building material collected by an asbestos inspector for laboratory analysis to determine asbestos content.

Bulky Waste: Large items of waste materials, such as appliances, furniture, large auto parts, trees, stumps.

Burial Ground (Graveyard): A disposal site for radioactive waste materials that uses earth or water as a shield.

Buy-Back Center: Facility where individuals or groups bring reyclables in return for payment.

By-product: Material, other than the principal product, generated as a consequence of an industrial process or as a breakdown product in a living system.

C

Cadmium (Cd): A heavy metal that accumulates in the environment.

Cancellation: Refers to Section 6 (b) of the Federal Insecticide, Fungicide and Rodenticide Act (FIFRA) which authorizes cancellation of a pesticide registration if unreasonable adverse effects to the environment and public health develop when a product is used according to widespread and commonly recognized practice, or if its labeling or other material required to be submitted does not comply with FIFRA provisions.

Cap: A layer of clay, or other impermeable material installed over the top of a closed landfill to prevent entry of rainwater and minimize leachate.

Capacity Assurance Plan: A statewide plan which supports a state's ability to manage the hazardous waste generated within its boundaries over a twenty year period.

Capillary Action: Movement of water through very small spaces due to molecular forces called capillary forces.

Capillary Fringe: The porous material just above the water table which may hold water by capillarity (a property of surface tension that draws water upwards) in the smaller void spaces.

Capillary Fringe: The zone above he water table within which the porous medium is saturated by water under less than atmospheric pressure.

Capture Efficiency: The fraction of organic vapors generated by a process that are directed to an abatement or recovery device.

Carbon Absorber: An add-on control device that uses activated carbon to absorb volatile organic compounds from a gas stream. (The VOCs are later recovered from the carbon.)

Carbon Adsorption: A treatment system that removes contaminants from ground water or surface water by forcing it through tanks containing activated carbon treated to attract the contaminants.

Carbon Monoxide (CO): A colorless, odorless, poisonous gas produced by incomplete fossil fuel combustion.

Carbon Tetrachloride (CC14): Compound consisting of one carbon atom ad four chlorine atoms, once widely used as a industrial raw material, as a solvent, and in the production of CFCs. Use as a solvent ended when it was discovered to be carcinogenic.

Carboxyhemoglobin: Hemoglobin in which the iron is bound to carbon monoxide(CO) instead of oxygen.

Carcinogen: Any substance that can cause or aggravate cancer.

Carrier: 1.The inert liquid or solid material in a pesticide product that serves as a delivery vehicle for the active ingredient. Carriers do not have toxic properties of their own. 2. Any material or system that can facilitate the movement of a pollutant into the body or cells.

Carrying Capacity: 1. In recreation management, the amount of use a recreation area can sustain without loss of quality. 2. In wildlife management, the maximum number of animals an area can support during a given period.

CAS Registration Number: A number assigned by the Chemical Abstract Service to identify a chemical.

Case Study: A brief fact sheet providing risk, cost, and performance information on alternative methods and other pollution prevention ideas, compliance initiatives, voluntary efforts, etc.

Cask: A thick-walled container (usually lead) used to transport radioactive material. Also called a coffin.

Catalyst: A substance that changes the speed or yield of a chemical reaction without being consumed or chemically changed by the chemical reaction.

Catalytic Converter: An air pollution abatement device that removes pollutants from motor vehicle exhaust, either by oxidizing them into carbon dioxide and water or reducing them to nitrogen.

Catalytic Incinerator: A control device that oxidizes volatile organic compounds (VOCs) by using a catalyst to promote the combustion process. Catalytic incinerators require lower temperatures than conventional thermal incinerators, thus saving fuel and other costs.

Categorical Exclusion: A class of actions which either individually or cumulatively would not have a significant effect on the human environment and therefore would not require preparation of an environmental assessment or environmental impact statement under the National Environmental Policy Act (NEPA).

Categorical Pretreatment Standard: A technology-based effluent limitation for an industrial facility discharging into a municipal sewer system. Analogous in stringency to Best Availability Technology (BAT) for direct dischargers.

Cathodic Protection: A technique to prevent corrosion of a metal surface by making it the cathode of an electrochemical cell.

Cavitation: The formation and collapse of gas pockets or bubbles on the blade of an impeller or the gate of a valve; collapse of these pockets or bubbles drives water with such force that it can cause pitting of the gate or valve surface.

Cells: 1. In solid waste disposal, holes where waste is dumped, compacted, and covered with layers of dirt on a daily basis. 2. The smallest structural part of living matter capable of functioning as an independent unit.

Cementitious: Densely packed and nonfibrous friable materials.

Central Collection Point: Location were a generator of regulated medical waste consolidates wastes originally generated at various locations in his facility. The wastes are gathered together for treatment on-site or for transportation elsewhere for treatment and/or disposal. This term could also apply to community hazardous waste collections, industrial and other waste management systems.

Centrifugal Collector: A mechanical system using centrifugal force to remove aerosols from a gas stream or to remove water from sludge.

CERCLIS: The federal Comprehensive Environmental Response, Compensation, and Liability Information System is a database that includes all sites which have been nominated for investigation by the Superfund program.

Channelization: Straightening and deepening streams so water will move faster, a marsh-drainage tactic that can interfere with waste assimilation capacity, disturb fish and wildlife habitats, and aggravate flooding.

Characteristic: Any one of the four categories used in defining hazardous waste: ignitability, corrosivity, reactivity, and toxicity.

Characterization of Ecological Effects: Part of ecological risk assessment that evaluates ability of a stressor to cause adverse effects under given circumstances.

Characterization of Exposure: Portion of an ecological risk assessment that evaluates interaction of a stressor with one or more ecological entities.

Check-Valve Tubing Pump: Water sampling tool also referred to as a water Pump.

Chemical Case: For purposes of review and regulation, the grouping of chemically similar pesticide active ingredients (*e.g.* salts and esters of the same chemical) into chemical cases.

Chemical Compound: A distinct and pure substance formed by the union or two or more elements in definite proportion by weight.

Chemical Element: A fundamental substance comprising one kind of atom; the simplest form of matter.

Chemical Oxygen Demand (COD): A measure of the oxygen required to oxidize all compounds, both organic and inorganic, in water.

Chemical Stressors: Chemicals released to the environment through industrial waste, auto emissions, pesticides, and other human activity that can cause illnesses and even death in plants and animals.

Chemical Treatment: Any one of a variety of technologies that use chemicals or a variety of chemical processes to treat waste.

Chemnet: Mutual aid network of chemical shippers and contractors that assigns a contracted emergency response company to provide technical support if a representative of the firm whose chemicals are involved in an incident is not readily available.

Chemosterilant: A chemical that controls pests by preventing reproduction.

Chemtrec: The industry-sponsored Chemical Transportation Emergency Center; provides information and/or emergency assistance to emergency responders.

Child Resistant Packaging (CRP): Packaging that protects children or adults from injury or illness resulting from accidental contact with or ingestion of residential pesticides that meet or exceed specific toxicity levels. Required by FIFRA regulations. Term is also used for protective packaging of medicines.

Chiller: A device that generates a cold liquid that is circulated through an air-handling unit's cooling coil to cool the air supplied to the building.

Chilling Effect: The lowering of the Earth's temperature because of increased particles in the air blocking the sun's rays. (See: greenhouse effect.)

Chisel Plowing: Preparing croplands by using a special implement that avoids complete inversion of the soil as in conventional plowing. Chisel plowing can leave a protective cover or crops residues on the soil surface to help prevent erosion and improve filtration.

Chlorinated Hydrocarbons: 1. Chemicals containing only chlorine, carbon, and hydrogen. These include a class of persistent, broad-spectrum insecticides that linger in the environment and accumulate in the food chain. Among them are DDT, aldrin, dieldrin, heptachlor, chlordane, lindane, endrin, Mirex, hexachloride, and toxaphene. Other examples include TCE, used as an industrial solvent. 2. Any chlorinated organic compounds including chlorinated solvents such as dichloromethane, trichloromethylene, chloroform.

Chlorinated Solvent: An organic solvent containing chlorine atoms(*e.g.* methylene chloride and 1,1,1-trichloromethane). Uses of chlorinated solvents are include aerosol spray containers, in highway paint, and dry cleaning fluids.

Chlorination: The application of chlorine to drinking water, sewage, or industrial waste to disinfect or to oxidize undesirable compounds.

Chlorinator: A device that adds chlorine, in gas or liquid form, to water or sewage to kill infectious bacteria.

Chlorine-Contact Chamber: That part of a water treatment plant where effluent is disinfected by chlorine.

Chlorofluorocarbons (CFCs): A family of inert, nontoxic, and easily liquefied chemicals used in refrigeration, air conditioning, packaging, insulation, or as solvents and aerosol propellants. Because CFCs are not destroyed in the lower atmosphere they drift into the upper atmosphere where their chlorine components destroy ozone. (See: fluorocarbons.)

Chlorophenoxy: A class of herbicides that may be found in domestic water supplies and cause adverse health effects.

Chlorosis: Discoloration of normally green plant parts caused by disease, lack of nutrients, or various air pollutants.

Cholinesterase: An enzyme found in animals that regulates nerve impulses by the inhibition of acetylcholine. Cholinesterase inhibition is associated with a variety of acute symptoms such as nausea, vomiting, blurred vision, stomach cramps, and rapid heart rate.

Chromium: (See: heavy metals.)

Chronic Effect: An adverse effect on a human or animal in which symptoms recur frequently or develop slowly over a long period of time.

Chronic Exposure: Multiple exposures occurring over an extended period of time or over a significant fraction of an animal's or human's lifetime (Usually seven years to a lifetime.)

Chronic Toxicity: The capacity of a substance to cause long-term poisonous health effects in humans, animals, fish, and other organisms. (See: acute toxicity.)

Circle of Influence: The circular outer edge of a depression produced in the water table by the pumping of water from a well. (See: cone of depression.)

Cistern: Small tank or storage facility used to store water for a home or farm; often used to store rain water.

Clarification: Clearing action that occurs during wastewater treatment when solids settle out. This is often aided by centrifugal action and chemically induced coagulation in wastewater.

Clarifier: A tank in which solids settle to the bottom and are subsequently removed as sludge.

Class I Area: Under the Clean Air Act. a Class I area is one in which visibility is protected more stringently than under the national ambient air quality standards; includes national parks, wilderness areas, monuments, and other areas of special national and cultural significance.

Class I Substance: One of several groups of chemicals with an ozone depletion potential of 0.2 or higher, including CFCS, Halons, Carbon Tetrachloride, and Methyl Chloroform (listed in the Clean Air Act), and HBFCs and Ethyl Bromide (added by EPA regulations). (See: Global warming potential.)

Class II Substance: A substance with an ozone depletion potential of less than 0.2. All HCFCs are currently included in this classification. (See: Global warming potential.)

Clay Soil: Soil material containing more than 40 percent clay, less than 45 percent sand, and less than 40 percent silt.

Clean Coal Technology: Any technology not in widespread use prior to the Clean Air Act Amendments of 1990. This Act will achieve significant reductions in pollutants associated with the burning of coal.

Clean Fuels: Blends or substitutes for gasoline fuels, including compressed natural gas, methanol, ethanol, and liquified petroleum gas.

Cleaner Technologies Substitutes Assessment: A document that systematically evaluates the relative risk, performance, and cost trade-offs of technological alternatives; serves as a repository for all the technical data (including methodology and results) developed by a DfE or other pollution prevention or education project.

Cleanup: Actions taken to deal with a release or threat of release of a hazardous substance that could affect humans and/or the environment. The term "cleanup" is sometimes used interchangeably with the terms remedial action, removal action, response action, or corrective action.

Clear Cut: Harvesting all the trees in one area at one time, a practice that can encourage fast rainfall or snowmelt runoff, erosion, sedimentation of streams and lakes, and flooding, and destroys vital habitat.

Clear Well: A reservoir for storing filtered water of sufficient quantity to prevent the need to vary the filtration rate with variations in demand. Also used to provide chlorine contact time for disinfection.

Climate Change (also referred to as 'global climate change'): The term 'climate change' is sometimes used to refer to all forms of climatic inconsistency, but because the Earth's climate is never static, the term is more properly used to imply a significant change from one climatic condition to another. In some cases, 'climate change' has been used synonymously with the term, 'global warming'; scientists however, tend to use the term in the wider sense to also include natural changes in climate. (See: global warming.)

Cloning: In biotechnology, obtaining a group of genetically identical cells from a single cell; making identical copies of a gene.

Closed-Loop Recycling: Reclaiming or reusing wastewater for non-potable purposes in an enclosed process.

Closure: The procedure a landfill operator must follow when a landfill reaches its legal capacity for solid ceasing acceptance of solid waste and placing a cap on the landfill site.

Co-fire: Burning of two fuels in the same combustion unit; *e.g.*, coal and natural gas, or oil and coal.

Coagulation: Clumping of particles in wastewater to settle out impurities, often induced by chemicals such as lime, alum, and iron salts.

Coal Cleaning Technology: A precombustion process by which coal is physically or chemically treated to remove some of its sulfur so as to reduce sulfur dioxide emissions.

Coal Gasification: Conversion of coal to a gaseous product by one of several available technologies.

Coastal Zone: Lands and waters adjacent to the coast that exert an influence on the uses of the sea and its ecology, or whose uses and ecology are affected by the sea.

Code of Federal Regulations (CFR): Document that codifies all rules of the executive departments and agencies of the federal government. It is divided into fifty volumes, known as titles. Title 40 of the CFR (referenced as 40 CFR) lists all environmental regulations.

Coefficient of Haze (COH): A measurement of visibility interference in the atmosphere.

Cogeneration: The consecutive generation of useful thermal and electric energy from the same fuel source.

Coke Oven: An industrial process which converts coal into coke, one of the basic materials used in blast furnaces for the conversion of iron ore into iron.

Cold Temperature CO: A standard for automobile emissions of carbon monoxide (CO) emissions to be met at a low temperature (*i.e.* 20 degrees Fahrenheit). Conventional automobile catalytic converters are not efficient in cold weather until they warm up.

Coliform Index: A rating of the purity of water based on a count of fecal bacteria.

Coliform Organism: Microorganisms found in the intestinal tract of humans and animals. Their presence in water indicates fecal pollution and potentially adverse contamination by pathogens.

Collector: Public or private hauler that collects nonhazardous waste and recyclable materials from residential, commercial, institutional and industrial sources.

Collector Sewers: Pipes used to collect and carry wastewater from individual sources to an interceptor sewer that will carry it to a treatment facility.

Colloids: Very small, finely divided solids (that do not dissolve) that remain dispersed in a liquid for a long time due to their small size and electrical charge.

Combined Sewer Overflows: Discharge of a mixture of storm water and domestic waste when the flow capacity of a sewer system is exceeded during rainstorms.

Combined Sewers: A sewer system that carries both sewage and storm-water runoff. Normally, its entire flow goes to a waste treatment plant, but during a heavy storm, the volume of water may be so great as to cause overflows of untreated mixtures of storm water and sewage into receiving waters. Storm-water runoff may also carry toxic chemicals from industrial areas or streets into the sewer system.

Combustion: 1. Burning, or rapid oxidation, accompanied by release of energy in the form of heat and light. 2. Refers to controlled burning of waste, in which heat chemically alters organic compounds, converting into stable inorganics such as carbon dioxide and water.

Combustion Chamber: The actual compartment where waste is burned in an incinerator.

Combustion Product: Substance produced during the burning or oxidation of a material.

Command Post: Facility located at a safe distance upwind from an accident site, where the on-scene coordinator, responders, and technical representatives make response decisions, deploy manpower and equipment, maintain liaison with news media, and handle communications.

Command-and-Control Regulations: Specific requirements prescribing how to comply with specific standards defining acceptable levels of pollution.

Comment Period: Time provided for the public to review and comment on a proposed EPA action or rulemaking after publication in the Federal Register.

Commercial Waste: All solid waste emanating from business establishments such as stores, markets, office buildings, restaurants, shopping centers, and theaters.

Commercial Waste Management Facility: A treatment, storage, disposal, or transfer facility which accepts waste from a variety of sources, as compared to a private facility which normally manages a limited waste stream generated by its own operations.

Commingled Recyclables: Mixed recyclables that are collected together.

Comminuter: A machine that shreds or pulverizes solids to make waste treatment easier.

Comminution: Mechanical shredding or pulverizing of waste. Used in both solid waste management and wastewater treatment.

Common Sense Initiative: Voluntary program to simplify environmental regulation to achieve cleaner, cheaper, smarter results, starting with six major industry sectors.

Community: In ecology, an assemblage of populations of different species within a specified location in space and time. Sometimes, a particular subgrouping may be specified, such as the fish community in a lake or the soil arthropod community in a forest.

Community Relations: The EPA effort to establish two-way communication with the public to create understanding of EPA programs and related actions, to ensure public input into decision-making processes related to affected communities, and to make certain that the Agency is aware of and responsive to public concerns. Specific community relations activities are required in relation to Superfund remedial actions.

Community Water System: A public water system which serves at least 15 service connections used by year-round residents or regularly serves at least 25 year-round residents.

Compact Fluorescent Lamp (CFL): Small fluorescent lamps used as more efficient alternatives to incandescent lighting. Also called PL, CFL, Twin-Tube, or BIAX lamps.

Compaction: Reduction of the bulk of solid waste by rolling and tamping.

Comparative Risk Assessment: Process that generally uses the judgement of experts to predict effects and set priorities among a wide range of environmental problems.

Complete Treatment: A method of treating water that consists of the addition of coagulant chemicals, flash mixing, coagulation-flocculation, sedimentation, and filtration. Also called conventional filtration.

Compliance Coal: Any coal that emits less than 1.2 pounds of sulfur dioxide per million Btu when burned. Also known as low sulfur coal. .

Compliance Coating: A coating whose volatile organic compound content does not exceed that allowed by regulation.

Compliance Cycle: The 9-year calendar year cycle, beginning January 1, 1993, during which public water systems must monitor. Each cycle consists of three 3-year compliance periods.

Compliance Monitoring: Collection and evaluation of data, including self-monitoring reports, and verification to show whether pollutant concentrations and loads contained in permitted discharges are in compliance with the limits and conditions specified in the permit.

Compliance Schedule: A negotiated agreement between a pollution source and a government agency that specifies dates and procedures by which a source will reduce emissions and, thereby, comply with a regulation.

Composite Sample: A series of water samples taken over a given period of time and weighted by flow rate.

Compost: A humus or soil-like material created from aerobic, microbial decomposition of organic materials such as food scraps, yard trimmings, and manure

Composting: The controlled biological decomposition of organic material in the presence of air to form a humus-like material. Controlled methods of composting include mechanical mixing and aerating, ventilating the materials by dropping them through a vertical series of aerated chambers, or placing the compost in piles out in the open air and mixing it or turning it periodically.

Composting Facilities: 1. An offsite facility where the organic component of municipal solid waste is decomposed under controlled conditions; 2.an aerobic process in which organic materials are ground or shredded and then decomposed to humus in windrow piles or in mechanical digesters, drums, or similar enclosures.

Compressed Natural Gas (CNG): An alternative fuel for motor vehicles; considered one of the cleanest because of low hydrocarbon emissions and its vapors are relatively non-ozone producing. However, vehicles fueled with CNG do emit a significant quantity of nitrogen oxides.

Concentration: The relative amount of a substance mixed with another substance. An example is five ppm of carbon monoxide in air or 1 mg/l of iron in water.

Condensate: 1. Liquid formed when warm landfill gas cools as it travels through a collection system. 2. Water created by cooling steam or water vapor.

Condensate Return System: System that returns the heated water condensing within steam piping to the boiler and thus saves energy.

Conditional Registration: Under special circumstances, the Federal Insecticide, Fungicide, and Rodenticide Act (FIFRA) permits registration of pesticide products that is "conditional" upon the submission of additional data. These special circumstances include a finding by the EPA Administrator that a new product or use of an existing pesticide will not significantly increase the risk of unreasonable adverse effects. A product containing a new (previously unregistered) active ingredient may be conditionally registered only if the Administrator finds that such conditional registration is in the public interest, that a reasonable time for conducting the additional studies has not elapsed, and the use of the pesticide for the period of conditional registration will not present an unreasonable risk.

Conditionally Exempt Generators (CE): Persons or enterprises which produce less than 220 pounds of hazardous waste per month. Exempt from most regulation, they are required merely to determine whether their waste is hazardous, notify appropriate state or local agencies, and ship it by an authorized transporter to a permitted facility for proper disposal. (See: small quantity generator.)

Conductance: A rapid method of estimating the dissolved solids content of water supply by determining the capacity of a water sample to carry an electrical current. Conductivity is a measure of the ability of a solution to carry and electrical current.

Conductivity: A measure of the ability of a solution to carry an electrical current.

Cone of Depression: A depression in the water table that develops around a pumped well.

Cone of Influence: The depression, roughly conical in shape, produced in a water table by the pumping of water from a well.

Cone Penterometer Testing (CPT): A direct push system used to measure lithology based on soil penetration resistance. Sensors in the tip of the cone of the DP rod measure tip resistance and sidewall friction, transmitting electrical signals to digital processing equipment on the ground surface. (See: direct push.)

Confidential Business Information (CBI): Material that contains trade secrets or commercial or financial information that has been claimed as confidential by its source (*e.g.* a pesticide or new chemical formulation registrant). EPA has special procedures for handling such information.

Confidential Statement of Formula (CSF): A list of the ingredients in a new pesticide or chemical formulation. The list is submitted at the time for application for registration or change in formulation.

Confined Aquifer: An aquifer in which ground water is confined under pressure which is significantly greater than atmospheric pressure.

Confluent Growth: A continuous bacterial growth covering all or part of the filtration area of a membrane filter in which the bacteria colonies are not discrete.

Consent Decree: A legal document, approved by a judge, that formalizes an agreement reached between EPA and potentially responsible parties (PRPs) through which PRPs will conduct all or part of a cleanup action at a Superfund site; cease or correct actions or processes that are polluting the environment; or otherwise comply with EPA initiated regulatory enforcement actions to resolve the contamination at the Superfund site involved. The consent decree describes the actions PRPs will take and may be subject to a public comment period.

Conservation: Preserving and renewing, when possible, human and natural resources. The use, protection, and improvement of natural resources according to principles that will ensure their highest economic or social benefits.

Conservation Easement: Easement restricting a landowner to land uses that that are compatible with long-term conservation and environmental values.

Constituent(s) of Concern: Specific chemicals that are identified for evaluation in the site assessment process

Construction and Demolition Waste: Waste building materials, dredging materials, tree stumps, and rubble resulting from construction, remodeling, repair, and demolition of homes, commercial buildings and other structures and pavements. May contain lead, asbestos, or other hazardous substances.

Construction Ban: If, under the Clean Air Act, EPA disapproves an area's planning requirements for correcting nonattainment, EPA can ban the construction or modification of any major stationary source of the pollutant for which the area is in nonattainment.

Consumptive Water Use: Water removed from available supplies without return to a water resources system, *e.g.* water used in manufacturing, agriculture, and food preparation.

Contact Pesticide: A chemical that kills pests when it touches them, instead of by ingestion. Also, soil that contains the minute skeletons of certain algae that scratch and dehydrate waxy-coated insects.

Contaminant: Any physical, chemical, biological, or radiological substance or matter that has an adverse effect on air, water, or soil.

Contamination: Introduction into water, air, and soil of microorganisms, chemicals, toxic substances, wastes, or wastewater in a concentration that makes the medium unfit for its next intended use. Also applies to surfaces of objects, buildings, and various household and agricultural use products.

Contamination Source Inventory: An inventory of contaminant sources within delineated State Water-Protection Areas. Targets likely sources for further investigation.

Contingency Plan: A document setting out an organized, planned, and coordinated course of action to be followed in case of a fire, explosion, or other accident that releases toxic chemicals, hazardous waste, or radioactive materials that threaten human health or the environment. (See: National Oil and Hazardous Substances Contingency Plan.)

Continuous Discharge: A routine release to the environment that occurs without interruption, except for infrequent shutdowns for maintenance, process changes, etc.

Continuous Sample: A flow of water, waste or other material from a particular place in a plant to the location where samples are collected for testing. May be used to obtain grab or composite samples.

Contour Plowing: Soil tilling method that follows the shape of the land to discourage erosion.

Contour Strip Farming: A kind of contour farming in which row crops are planted in strips, between alternating strips of close-growing, erosion-resistant forage crops.

Contract Labs: Laboratories under contract to EPA, which analyze samples taken from waste, soil, air, and water or carry out research projects.

Control Technique Guidelines (CTG): EPA documents designed to assist state and local pollution authorities to achieve and maintain air quality standards for certain sources (*e.g.* organic emissions from solvent metal cleaning known as degreasing) through reasonably available control technologies (RACT).

Controlled Reaction: A chemical reaction under temperature and pressure conditions maintained within safe limits to produce a desired product or process.

Conventional Filtration: (See: complete treatment.)

Conventional Pollutants: Statutorily listed pollutants understood well by scientists. These may be in the form of organic waste, sediment, acid, bacteria, viruses, nutrients, oil and grease, or heat.

Conventional Site Assessment: Assessment in which most of the sample analysis and interpretation of data is completed off-site; process usually requires repeated mobilization of equipment and staff in order to fully determine the extent of contamination.

Conventional Systems: Systems that have been traditionally used to collect municipal wastewater in gravity sewers and convey it to a central primary or secondary treatment plant prior to discharge to surface waters.

Conventional Tilling: Tillage operations considered standard for a specific location and crop and that tend to bury the crop residues; usually considered as a base for determining the cost effectiveness of control practices.

Conveyance Loss: Water loss in pipes, channels, conduits, ditches by leakage or evaporation.

Cooling Electricity Use: Amount of electricity used to meet the building cooling load. (See: building cooling load.)

Cooling Tower: A structure that helps remove heat from water used as a coolant; *e.g.*, in electric power generating plants.

Cooling Tower: Device which dissipates the heat from water-cooled systems by spraying the water through streams of rapidly moving air.

Cooperative Agreement: An assistance agreement whereby EPA transfers money, property, services or anything of value to a state, university, non-profit, or not-for-profit organization for the accomplishment of authorized activities or tasks.

Core: The uranium-containing heart of a nuclear reactor, where energy is released.

Core Program Cooperative Agreement: An assistance agreement whereby EPA supports states or tribal governments with funds to help defray the cost of non-item-specific administrative and training activities.

Corrective Action: EPA can require treatment, storage and disposal (TSDF) facilities handling hazardous waste to undertake corrective actions to clean up spills resulting from failure to follow hazardous waste management procedures or other mistakes. The process includes cleanup procedures designed to guide TSDFs toward in spills.

Corrosion: The dissolution and wearing away of metal caused by a chemical reaction such as between water and the pipes, chemicals touching a metal surface, or contact between two metals.

Corrosive: A chemical agent that reacts with the surface of a material causing it to deteriorate or wear away.

Cost/Benefit Analysis: A quantitative evaluation of the costs which would have incurred by implementing an environmental regulation versus the overall benefits to society of the proposed action.

Cost Recovery: A legal process by which potentially responsible parties who contributed to contamination at a Superfund site can be required to reimburse the Trust Fund for money spent during any cleanup actions by the federal government.

Cost Sharing: A publicly financed program through which society, as a beneficiary of environmental protection, shares part of the cost of pollution control with those who must actually install the controls. In Superfund, for example, the government may pay part of the cost of a cleanup action with those responsible for the pollution paying the major share.

Cost-Effective Alternative: An alternative control or corrective method identified after analysis as being the best available in terms of reliability, performance, and cost. Although costs are one important consideration, regulatory and compliance analysis does not require EPA to choose the least expensive alternative. For example, when selecting or approving a method for cleaning up a Superfund site, the Agency balances costs with the long-term effectiveness of the methods proposed and the potential danger posed by the site.

Cover Crop: A crop that provides temporary protection for delicate seedlings and/or provides a cover canopy for seasonal soil protection and improvement between normal crop production periods.

Cover Material: Soil used to cover compacted solid waste in a sanitary landfill.

Cradle-to-Grave or Manifest System: A procedure in which hazardous materials are identified and followed as they are produced, treated, transported, and disposed of by a series of permanent, linkable, descriptive documents (*e.g.* manifests). Commonly referred to as the cradle-to-grave system.

Criteria: Descriptive factors taken into account by EPA in setting standards for various pollutants. These factors are used to determine limits on allowable concentration levels, and to limit the number of violations per year. When issued by EPA, the criteria provide guidance to the states on how to establish their standards.

Criteria Pollutants: The 1970 amendments to the Clean Air Act required EPA to set National Ambient Air Quality Standards for certain pollutants known to be hazardous to human health. EPA has identified and set standards to protect human health and welfare for six pollutants: ozone, carbon monoxide, total suspended particulates, sulfur dioxide, lead, and nitrogen oxide. The term, "criteria pollutants" derives from the requirement that EPA must describe the characteristics and potential health and welfare effects of these pollutants. It is on the basis of these criteria that standards are set or revised.

Critical Effect: The first adverse effect, or its known precursor, that occurs as a dose rate increases. Designation is based on evaluation of overall database.

Crop Consumptive Use: The amount of water transpired during plant growth plus what evaporated from the soil surface and foliage in the crop area.

Crop Rotation: Planting a succession of different crops on the same land rea as opposed to planting the same crop time after time.

Cross Contamination: The movement of underground contaminants from one level or area to another due to invasive subsurface activities.

Cross-Connection: Any actual or potential connection between a drinking water system and an unapproved water supply or other source of contamination.

Crumb Rubber: Ground rubber fragments the size of sand or silt used in rubber or plastic products, or processed further into reclaimed rubber or asphalt products.

Cryptosporidium: A protozoan microbe associated with the disease cryptosporidiosis in man. The disease can be transmitted through ingestion of drinking water, person-to-person contact, or other pathways, and can cause acute diarrhea, abdominal pain, vomiting, fever, and can be fatal as it was in the Milwaukee episode.

Cubic Feet Per Minute (CFM): A measure of the volume of a substance flowing through air within a fixed period of time. With regard to indoor air, refers to the amount of air, in cubic feet, that is exchanged with outdoor air in a minute's time; *i.e.* the air exchange rate.

Cullet: Crushed glass.

Cultural Eutrophication: Increasing rate at which water bodies "die" by pollution from human activities.

Cultures and Stocks: Infectious agents and associated biologicals including cultures from medical and pathological laboratories; cultures and stocks of infectious agents from research and industrial laboratories; waste from the production of biologicals; discarded live and attenuated vaccines; and culture dishes and devices used to transfer, inoculate, and mix cultures. (See: regulated medical waste.)

Cumulative Ecological Risk Assessment: Consideration of the total ecological risk from multiple stressors to a given eco-zone.

Cumulative Exposure: The sum of exposures of an organism to a pollutant over a period of time.

Cumulative Working Level Months (CWLM): The sum of lifetime exposure to radon working levels expressed in total working level months.

Curb Stop: A water service shutoff valve located in a water service pipe near the curb and between the water main and the building.

Curbside Collection: Method of collecting recyclable materials at homes, community districts or businesses.

Cutie-Pie: An instrument used to measure radiation levels.

Cuttings: Spoils left by conventional drilling with hollow stem auger or rotary drilling equipment.

Cyclone Collector: A device that uses centrifugal force to remove large particles from polluted air.

D

Data Call-In: A part of the Office of Pesticide Programs (OPP) process of developing key required test data, especially on the long-term, chronic effects of existing pesticides, in advance of scheduled Registration Standard reviews. Data Call-In from manufacturers is an adjunct of the Registration Standards program intended to expedite re-registration.

Data Quality Objectives (DQOs): Qualitative and quantitative statements of the overall level of uncertainty that a decision-maker will accept in results or decisions based on environmental data. They provide the statistical framework for planning and managing environmental data operations consistent with user's needs.

Day Tank: Another name for de-aerating tank. (See: age tank.)

DDT: The first chlorinated hydrocarbon insecticide chemical name: Dichloro-Diphenyl-Trichloroethane. It has a half-life of 15 years and can collect in fatty tissues of certain animals. EPA banned registration and interstate sale of DDT for virtually all but emergency uses in the United States in 1972 because of its persistence in the environment and accumulation in the food chain.

Dead End: The end of a water main which is not connected to other parts of the distribution system.

Deadmen: Anchors drilled or cemented into the ground to provide additional reactive mass for DP sampling rigs.

Decant: To draw off the upper layer of liquid after the heaviest material (a solid or another liquid) has settled.

Decay Products: Degraded radioactive materials, often referred to as "daughters" or "progeny"; radon decay products of most concern from a public health standpoint are polonium-214 and polonium-218.

Dechlorination: Removal of chlorine from a substance.

Decomposition: The breakdown of matter by bacteria and fungi, changing the chemical makeup and physical appearance of materials.

Decontamination: Removal of harmful substances such as noxious chemicals, harmful bacteria or other organisms, or radioactive material from exposed individuals, rooms and furnishings in buildings, or the exterior environment.

Deep-Well Injection: Deposition of raw or treated, filtered hazardous waste by pumping it into deep wells, where it is contained in the pores of permeable subsurface rock.

Deflocculating Agent: A material added to a suspension to prevent settling.

Defluoridation: The removal of excess flouride in drinking water to prevent the staining of teeth.

Defoliant: An herbicide that removes leaves from trees and growing plants.

Degasification: A water treatment that removes dissolved gases from the water.

Degree-Day: A rough measure used to estimate the amount of heating required in a given area; is defined as the difference between the mean daily temperature and 65 degrees Fahrenheit. Degree days are also calculated to estimate cooling requirements.

Delegated State: A state (or other governmental entity such as a tribal government) that has received authority to administer an environmental regulatory program in lieu of a federal counterpart. As used in connection with NPDES, UIC, and PWS programs, the term does not connote any transfer of federal authority to a state.

Delist: Use of the petition process to have a facility's toxic designation rescinded.

Demand-side Waste Management: Prices whereby consumers use purchasing decisions to communicate to product manufacturers that they prefer environmentally sound products packaged with the least amount of waste, made from recycled or recyclable materials, and containing no hazardous substances.

Demineralization: A treatment process that removes dissolved minerals from water.

Denitrification: The biological reduction of nitrate to nitrogen gas by denitrifying bacteria in soil.

Dense Non-Aqueous Phase Liquid (DNAPL): Non-aqueous phase liquids such as chlorinated hydrocarbon solvents or petroleum fractions with a specific gravity greater than 1.0 that sink through the water column until they reach a confining layer. Because they are at the bottom of aquifers instead of floating on the water table, typical monitoring wells do not indicate their presence.

Density: A measure of how heavy a specific volume of a solid, liquid, or gas is in comparison to water. depending on the chemical.

Depletion Curve: In hydraulics, a graphical representation of water depletion from storage-stream channels, surface soil, and groundwater. A depletion curve can be drawn for base flow, direct runoff, or total flow.

Depressurization: A condition that occurs when the air pressure inside a structure is lower that the air pressure outdoors. Depressurization can occur when household appliances such as fireplaces or furnaces, that consume or exhaust house air, are not supplied with enough makeup air. Radon may be drawn into a house more rapidly under depressurized conditions.

Dermal Absorption/Penetration: Process by which a chemical penetrates the skin and enters the body as an internal dose.

Dermal Exposure: Contact between a chemical and the skin.

Dermal Toxicity: The ability of a pesticide or toxic chemical to poison people or animals by contact with the skin. (See: contact pesticide.)

DES: A synthetic estrogen, diethylstilbestrol is used as a growth stimulant in food animals. Residues in meat are thought to be carcinogenic.

Desalination: [Desalinization] (1) Removing salts from ocean or brackish water by using various technologies. (2) Removal of salts from soil by artificial means, usually leaching.

Desiccant: A chemical agent that absorbs moisture; some desiccants are capable of drying out plants or insects, causing death.

Design Capacity: The average daily flow that a treatment plant or other facility is designed to accommodate.

Design Value: The monitored reading used by EPA to determine an area's air quality status; *e.g.*, for ozone, the fourth highest reading measured over the most recent three years is the design value.

Designated Pollutant: An air pollutant which is neither a criteria nor hazardous pollutant, as described in the Clean Air Act, but for which new source performance standards exist. The Clean Air Act does require states to control these pollutants, which include acid mist, total reduced sulfur (TRS), and fluorides.

Designated Uses: Those water uses identified in state water quality standards that must be achieved and maintained as required under the Clean Water Act. Uses can include cold water fisheries, public water supply, and irrigation.

Designer Bugs: Popular term for microbes developed through biotechnology that can degrade specific toxic chemicals at their source in toxic waste dumps or in ground water.

Destination Facility: The facility to which regulated medical waste is shipped for treatment and destruction, incineration, and/or disposal.

Destratification: Vertical mixing within a lake or reservoir to totally or partially eliminate separate layers of temperature, plant, or animal life.

Destroyed Medical Waste: Regulated medical waste that has been ruined, torn apart, or mutilated through thermal treatment, melting, shredding, grinding, tearing, or breaking, so that it is no longer generally recognized as medical waste, but has not yet been treated (excludes compacted regulated medical waste).

Destruction and Removal Efficiency (DRE): A percentage that represents the number of molecules of a compound removed or destroyed in an incinerator relative to the number of molecules entering the system (*e.g.* a DRE of 99.99 percent means that 9,999 molecules are destroyed for every 10,000 that enter; 99.99 percent is known as "four nines." For some pollutants, the RCRA removal requirement may be as stringent as "six nines").

Destruction Facility: A facility that destroys regulated medical waste.

Desulfurization: Removal of sulfur from fossil fuels to reduce pollution.

Detectable Leak Rate: The smallest leak (from a storage tank), expressed in terms of gallons- or liters-per-hour, that a test can reliably discern with a certain probability of detection or false alarm.

Detection Criterion: A predetermined rule to ascertain whether a tank is leaking or not. Most volumetric tests use a threshold value as the detection criterion. (See: volumetric tank tests.)

Detection Limit: The lowest concentration of a chemical that can reliably be distinguished from a zero concentration.

Detention Time: 1. The theoretical calculated time required for a small amount of water to pass through a tank at a given rate of flow. 2. The actual time that a small amount of water is in a settling basin, flocculating basin, or rapid-mix chamber. 3. In storage reservoirs, the length of time water will be held before being used.

Detergent: Synthetic washing agent that helps to remove dirt and oil. Some contain compounds which kill useful bacteria and encourage algae growth when they are in wastewater that reaches receiving waters.

Development Effects: Adverse effects such as altered growth, structural abnormality, functional deficiency, or death observed in a developing organism.

Dewater: 1. Remove or separate a portion of the water in a sludge or slurry to dry the sludge so it can be handled and disposed of. 2. Remove or drain the water from a tank or trench.

Diatomaceous Earth (Diatomite): A chalk-like material (fossilized diatoms) used to filter out solid waste in wastewater treatment plants; also used as an active ingredient in some powdered pesticides.

Diazinon: An insecticide. In 1986, EPA banned its use on open areas such as sod farms and golf courses because it posed a danger to migratory birds. The ban did not apply to agricultural, home lawn or commercial establishment uses.

Dibenzofurans: A group of organic compounds, some of which are toxic.

Dicofol: A pesticide used on citrus fruits.

Diffused Air: A type of aeration that forces oxygen into sewage by pumping air through perforated pipes inside a holding tank.

Diffusion: The movement of suspended or dissolved particles (or molecules) from a more concentrated to a less concentrated area. The process tends to distribute the particles or molecules more uniformly.

Digester: In wastewater treatment, a closed tank; in solid-waste conversion, a unit in which bacterial action is induced and accelerated in order to break down organic matter and establish the proper carbon to nitrogen ratio.

Digestion: The biochemical decomposition of organic matter, resulting in partial gasification, liquefaction, and mineralization of pollutants.

Dike: A low wall that can act as a barrier to prevent a spill from spreading.

Diluent: Any liquid or solid material used to dilute or carry an active ingredient.

Dilution Ratio: The relationship between the volume of water in a stream and the volume of incoming water. It affects the ability of the stream to assimilate waste.

Dimictic: Lakes and reservoirs that freeze over and normally go through two stratifications and two mixing cycles a year.

Dinocap: A fungicide used primarily by apple growers to control summer diseases. EPA proposed restrictions on its use in 1986 when laboratory tests found it caused birth defects in rabbits.

Dinoseb: A herbicide that is also used as a fungicide and insecticide. It was banned by EPA in 1986 because it posed the risk of birth defects and sterility.

Dioxin: Any of a family of compounds known chemically as dibenzo-p-dioxins. Concern about them arises from their potential toxicity as contaminants in commercial products. Tests on laboratory animals indicate that it is one of the more toxic anthropogenic (man-made) compounds.

Direct Discharger: A municipal or industrial facility which introduces pollution through a defined conveyance or system such as outlet pipes; a point source.

Direct Filtration: A method of treating water which consists of the addition of coagulent chemicals, flash mixing, coagulation, minimal flocculation, and filtration. Sedimentation is not uses.

Direct Push: Technology used for performing subsurface investigations by driving, pushing, and/or vibrating small-diameter hollow steel rods into the ground/ Also known as direct drive, drive point, or push technology.

Direct Runoff: Water that flows over the ground surface or through the ground directly into streams, rivers, and lakes.

Discharge: Flow of surface water in a stream or canal or the outflow of ground water from a flowing artesian well, ditch, or spring. Can also apply tp discharge of liquid effluent from a facility or to chemical emissions into the air through designated venting mechanisms.

Disinfectant: A chemical or physical process that kills pathogenic organisms in water, air, or on surfaces. Chlorine is often used to disinfect sewage treatment effluent, water supplies, wells, and swimming pools.

Disinfectant By-Product: A compound formed by the reaction of a disinfenctant such as chlorine with organic material in the water supply; a chemical byproduct of the disinfection process.

Disinfectant Time: The time it takes water to move from the point of disinfectant application (or the previous point of residual disinfectant measurement) to a point before or at the point where the residual disinfectant is measured. In pipelines, the time is calculated by dividing the internal volume of the pipe by he maximum hourly flow rate; within mixing basins and storage reservoirs it is determined by tracer studies of an equivalent demonstration.

Dispersant: A chemical agent used to break up concentrations of organic material such as spilled oil.

Displacement Savings: Saving realized by displacing purchases of natural gas or electricity from a local utility by using landfill gas for power and heat.

Disposables: Consumer products, other items, and packaging used once or a few times and discarded.

Disposal: Final placement or destruction of toxic, radioactive, or other wastes; surplus or banned pesticides or other chemicals; polluted soils; and drums containing hazardous materials from removal actions or accidental releases. Disposal may be accomplished through use of approved secure landfills, surface impoundments, land farming, deep-well injection, ocean dumping, or incineration.

Disposal Facilities: Repositories for solid waste, including landfills and combustors intended for permanent containment or destruction of waste materials. Excludes transfer stations and composting facilities.

Dissolved Oxygen (DO): The oxygen freely available in water, vital to fish and other aquatic life and for the prevention of odors. DO levels are considered a most important indicator of a water body's ability to support desirable aquatic life. Secondary and advanced waste treatment are generally designed to ensure adequate DO in waste-receiving waters.

Dissolved Solids: Disintegrated organic and inorganic material in water. Excessive amounts make water unfit to drink or use in industrial processes.

Distillation: The act of purifying liquids through boiling, so that the steam or gaseous vapors condense to a pure liquid. Pollutants and contaminants may remain in a concentrated residue.

Disturbance: Any event or series of events that disrupt ecosystem, community, or population structure and alters the physical environment.

Diversion: 1. Use of part of a stream flow as water supply. 2. A channel with a supporting ridge on the lower side constructed across a slope to divert water at a non-erosive velocity to sites where it can be used and disposed of.

Diversion Rate: The percentage of waste materials diverted from traditional disposal such as landfilling or incineration to be recycled, composted, or re-used.

DNA Hybridization: Use of a segment of DNA, called a DNA probe, to identify its complementary DNA; used to detect specific genes.

Dobson Unit (DU): Units of ozone level measurement. measurement of ozone levels. If, for example, 100 DU of ozone were brought to the earth's surface they would form a layer one millimeter thick. Ozone levels vary geographically, even in the absence of ozone depletion.

Domestic Application: Pesticide application in and around houses, office buildings, motels, and other living or working areas.(See: residential use.)

Dosage/Dose: 1. The actual quantity of a chemical administered to an organism or to which it is exposed. 2. The amount of a substance that reaches a specific tissue (*e.g.* the liver). 3. The amount of a substance available for interaction with metabolic processes after crossing the outer boundary of an organism. (See: absorbed dose, administered dose, applied dose, potential dose.)

Dose Equivalent: The product of the absorbed dose from ionizing radiation and such factors as account for biological differences due to the type of radiation and its distribution in the body in the body.

Dose Rate: In exposure assessment, dose per time unit (*e.g.* mg/day), sometimes also called dosage.

Dose Response: Shifts in toxicological responses of an individual (such as alterations in severity) or populations (such as alterations in incidence) that are related to changes in the dose of any given substance.

Dose Response Curve: Graphical representation of the relationship between the dose of a stressor and the biological response thereto.

Dose-Response Assessment: 1. Estimating the potency of a chemical. 2. In exposure assessment, the process of determining the relationship between the dose of a stressor and a specific biological response. 3. Evaluating the quantitative relationship between dose and toxicological responses.

Dose-Response Relationship: The quantitative relationship between the amount of exposure to a substance and the extent of toxic injury or disease produced.

Dosimeter: An instrument to measure dosage; many so-called dosimeters actually measure exposure rather than dosage. Dosimetry is the process or technology of measuring and/or estimating dosage.

DOT Reportable Quantity: The quantity of a substance specified in a U.S. Department of Transportation regulation that triggers labeling, packaging and other requirements related to shipping such substances.

Downgradient: The direction that groundwater flows; similar to "downstream" for surface water.

Downstream Processors: Industries dependent on crop production (*e.g.* canneries and food processors).

DP Hole: Hole in the ground made with DP equipment. (See: direct push.)

Draft: 1. The act of drawing or removing water from a tank or reservoir. 2. The water which is drawn or removed.

Draft Permit: A preliminary permit drafted and published by EPA; subject to public review and comment before final action on the application.

Drainage: Improving the productivity of agricultural land by removing excess water from the soil by such means as ditches or subsurface drainage tiles.

Drainage Basin: The area of land that drains water, sediment, and dissolved materials to a common outlet at some point along a stream channel.

Drainage Well: A well drilled to carry excess water off agricultural fields. Because they act as a funnel from the surface to the groundwater below. Drainage wells can contribute to groundwater pollution.

Drawdown: 1. The drop in the water table or level of water in the ground when water is being pumped from a well. 2. The amount of water used from a tank or reservoir. 3. The drop in the water level of a tank or reservoir.

Dredging: Removal of mud from the bottom of water bodies. This can disturb the ecosystem and causes silting that kills aquatic life. Dredging of contaminated muds can expose biota to heavy metals and other toxics. Dredging activities may be subject to regulation under Section 404 of the Clean Water Act.

Drilling Fluid: Fluid used to lubricate the bit and convey drill cuttings to the surface with rotary drilling equipment. Usually composed of bentonite slurry or muddy water. Can become contaminated, leading to cross contamination, and may require special disposal. Not used with DP methods.

Drinking Water Equivalent Level: Protective level of exposure related to potentially non carcinogenic effects of chemicals that are also known to cause cancer.

Drinking Water State Revolving Fund: The Fund provides capitalization grants to states to develop drinking water revolving loan funds to help finance system infrastructure improvements, assure source-water protection, enhance operation and management of drinking-water systems, and otherwise promote local water-system compliance and protection of public health.

Drive Casing: Heavy duty steel casing driven along with the sampling tool in cased DP systems. Keeps the hole open between sampling runs and is not removed until last sample has been collected.

Drive Point Profiler: An exposed groundwater DP system used to collect multiple depth-discrete groundwater samples. Ports in the tip of the probe connect to an internal stainless steel or teflon tube that extends to the surface. Samples are collected via suction or airlift methods. Deionized water is pumped down through the ports to prevent plugging while driving the tool to the next sampling depth.

Drop-off: Recyclable materials collection method in which individuals bring them to a designated collection site.

Dual-Phase Extraction: Active withdrawal of both liquid and gas phases from a well usually involving the use of a vacuum pump.

Dump: A site used to dispose of solid waste without environmental controls.

Duplicate: A second aliquot or sample that is treated the same as the original sample in order to determine the precision of the analytical method. (See: aliquot.)

Dustfall Jar: An open container used to collect large particles from the air for measurement and analysis.

Dynamometer. A device used to place a load on an engine and measure its performance.

Dystrophic Lakes: Acidic, shallow bodies of water that contain much humus and/or other organic matter; contain many plants but few fish.

E

Ecological Entity: In ecological risk assessment, a general term referring to a species, a group of species, an ecosystem function or characteristic, or a specific habitat or biome.

Ecological/Environmental Sustainability: Maintenance of ecosystem components and functions for future generations.

Ecological Exposure: Exposure of a non-human organism to a stressor.

Ecological Impact: The effect that a man-caused or natural activity has on living organisms and their non-living (abiotic) environment.

Ecological Indicator: A characteristic of an ecosystem that is related to, or derived from, a measure of biotic or abiotic variable, that can provide quantitative information on ecological structure and function. An indicator can contribute to a measure of integrity and sustainability.

Ecological Integrity: A living system exhibits integrity if, when subjected to disturbance, it sustains and organizes self-correcting ability to recover toward a biomass end-state that is normal for that system. End-states other than the pristine or naturally whole may be accepted as normal and good.

Ecological Risk Assessment: The application of a formal framework, analytical process, or model to estimate the effects of human actions(s) on a natural resource and to interpret the significance of those effects in light of the uncertainties identified in each component of the assessment process. Such analysis includes initial hazard identification, exposure and dose-response assessments, and risk characterization.

Ecology: The relationship of living things to one another and their environment, or the study of such relationships.

Economic Poisons: Chemicals used to control pests and to defoliate cash crops such as cotton.

Ecosphere: The "bio-bubble" that contains life on earth, in surface waters, and in the air. (See: biosphere.)

Ecosystem: The interacting system of a biological community and its non-living environmental surroundings.

Ecosystem Structure: Attributes related to the instantaneous physical state of an ecosystem; examples include species population density, species richness or evenness, and standing crop biomass.

Ecotone: A habitat created by the juxtaposition of distinctly different habitats; an edge habitat; or an ecological zone or boundary where two or more ecosystems meet.

Effluent: Wastewater—treated or untreated—that flows out of a treatment plant, sewer, or industrial outfall. Generally refers to wastes discharged into surface waters.

Effluent Guidelines: Technical EPA documents which set effluent limitations for given industries and pollutants.

Effluent Limitation: Restrictions established by a state or EPA on quantities, rates, and concentrations in wastewater discharges.

Effluent Standard: (See: effluent limitation.)

Ejector: A device used to disperse a chemical solution into water being treated.

Electrodialysis: A process that uses electrical current applied to permeable membranes to remove minerals from water. Often used to desalinize salty or brackish water.

Electromagnetic Geophysical Methods: Ways to measure subsurface conductivity via low frequency electromagnetic induction.

Electrostatic Precipitator (ESP): A device that removes particles from a gas stream (smoke) after combustion occurs. The ESP imparts an electrical charge to the particles, causing them to adhere to metal plates inside the precipitator. Rapping on the plates causes the particles to fall into a hopper for disposal.

Eligible Costs: The construction costs for wastewater treatment works upon which EPA grants are based.

EMAP Data: Environmental monitoring data collected under the auspices of the Environmental Monitoring and Assessment Program. All EMAP data share the common attribute of being of known quality, having been collected in the context of explicit data quality objectives (DQOs) and a consistent quality assurance program.

Emergency and Hazardous Chemical Inventory: An annual report by facilities having one or more extremely hazardous substances or hazardous chemicals above certain weight limits.

Emergency (Chemical): A situation created by an accidental release or spill of hazardous chemicals that poses a threat to the safety of workers, residents, the environment, or property.

Emergency Episode: (See: air pollution episode.)

Emergency Exemption: Provision in FIFRA under which EPA can grant temporary exemption to a state or another federal agency to allow the use of a pesticide product not registered for that particular use. Such actions involve unanticipated and/or severe pest problems where there is not time or interest by a manufacturer to register the product for that use. (Registrants cannot apply for such exemptions.)

Emergency Removal Action: 1. Steps take to remove contaminated materials that pose imminent threats to local residents (*e.g.* removal of leaking drums or the excavation of explosive waste.) 2. The state record of such removals.

Emergency Response Values: Concentrations of chemicals, published by various groups, defining acceptable levels for short-term exposures in emergencies.

Emergency Suspension: Suspension of a pesticide product registration due to an imminent hazard. The action immediately halts distribution, sale, and sometimes actual use of the pesticide involved.

Emission: Pollution discharged into the atmosphere from smokestacks, other vents, and surface areas of commercial or industrial facilities; from residential chimneys; and from motor vehicle, locomotive, or aircraft exhausts.

Emission Cap: A limit designed to prevent projected growth in emissions from existing and future stationary sources from eroding any mandated reductions. Generally, such provisions require that any emission growth from facilities under the restrictions be offset by equivalent reductions at other facilities under the same cap.

Emission Factor: The relationship between the amount of pollution produced and the amount of raw material processed. For example, an emission factor for a blast furnace making iron would be the number of pounds of particulates per ton of raw materials.

Emission Inventory: A listing, by source, of the amount of air pollutants discharged into the atmosphere of a community; used to establish emission standards.

Emission Standard: The maximum amount of air polluting discharge legally allowed from a single source, mobile or stationary.

Emissions Trading: The creation of surplus emission reductions at certain stacks, vents or similar emissions sources and the use of this surplus to meet or redefine pollution requirements applicable to other emissions sources. This allows one source to increase emissions when another source reduces them, maintaining an overall constant emission level. Facilities that reduce emissions substantially may "bank" their "credits" or sell them to other facilities or industries.

Emulsifier: A chemical that aids in suspending one liquid in another. Usually an organic chemical in an aqueous solution.

Encapsulation: The treatment of asbestos-containing material with a liquid that covers the surface with a protective coating or embeds fibers in an adhesive matrix to prevent their release into the air.

Enclosure: Putting an airtight, impermeable, permanent barrier around asbestos-containing materials to prevent the release of asbestos fibers into the air.

End User: Consumer of products for the purpose of recycling. Excludes products for re-use or combustion for energy recovery.

End-of-the-pipe: Technologies such as scrubbers on smokestacks and catalytic convertors on automobile tailpipes that reduce emissions of pollutants after they have formed.

End-use Product: A pesticide formulation for field or other end use. The label has instructions for use or application to control pests or regulate plant growth. The term excludes products used to formulate other pesticide products.

Endangered Species: Animals, birds, fish, plants, or other living organisms threatened with extinction by anthropogenic (man-caused) or other natural changes in their environment. Requirements for declaring a species endangered are contained in the Endangered Species Act.

Endangerment Assessment: A study to determine the nature and extent of contamination at a site on the National Priorities List and the risks posed to public health or the environment. EPA or the state conducts the study when a legal action is to be taken to direct potentially responsible parties to clean up a site or pay for it. An endangerment assessment supplements a remedial investigation.

Endrin: A pesticide toxic to freshwater and marine aquatic life that produces adverse health effects in domestic water supplies.

Energy Management System: A control system capable of monitoring environmental and system loads and adjusting HVAC operations accordingly in order to conserve energy while maintaining comfort.

Energy Recovery: Obtaining energy from waste through a variety of processes (*e.g.* combustion).

Enforceable Requirements: Conditions or limitations in permits issued under the Clean Water Act Section 402 or 404 that, if violated, could result in the issuance of a compliance order or initiation of a civil or criminal action under federal or applicable state laws. If a permit has not been issued, the term includes any requirement which, in the Regional Administrator's judgement, would be included in the permit when issued. Where no permit applies, the term includes any requirement which the RA determines is necessary for the best practical waste treatment technology to meet applicable criteria.

Enforcement: EPA, state, or local legal actions to obtain compliance with environmental laws, rules, regulations, or agreements and/or obtain penalties or criminal sanctions for violations. Enforcement procedures may vary, depending on the requirements of different environmental laws and related implementing regulations. Under CERCLA, for example, EPA will seek to require potentially responsible parties to clean up a Superfund site, or pay for the cleanup, whereas under the Clean Air Act the Agency may invoke sanctions against cities failing to meet ambient air quality standards that could prevent certain types of construction or federal funding. In other situations, if investigations by EPA and state agencies uncover willful violations, criminal trials and penalties are sought.

Enforcement Decision Document (EDD): A document that provides an explanation to the public of EPA's selection of the cleanup alternative at enforcement sites on the National Priorities List. Similar to a Record of Decision.

Engineered Controls: Method of managing environmental and health risks by placing a barrier between the contamination and the rest of the site, thus limiting exposure pathways.

Enhanced Inspection and Maintenance (I&M): An improved automobile inspection and maintenance program—aimed at reducing automobile emissions—that contains, at a minimum, more vehicle types and model years, tighter inspection, and better management practices. It may also include annual computerized or centralized inspections, under-the-hood inspection—for signs of tampering with pollution control equipment—and increased repair waiver cost.

Enrichment: The addition of nutrients (*e.g.* nitrogen, phosphorus, carbon compounds) from sewage effluent or agricultural runoff to surface water, greatly increases the growth potential for algae and other aquatic plants.

Entrain: To trap bubbles in water either mechanically through turbulence or chemically through a reaction.

Environment: The sum of all external conditions affecting the life, development and survival of an organism.

Environmental Assessment: An environmental analysis prepared pursuant to the National Environmental Policy Act to determine whether a federal action would significantly affect the environment and thus require a more detailed environmental impact statement.

Environmental Audit: An independent assessment of the current status of a party's compliance with applicable environmental requirements or of a party's environmental compliance policies, practices, and controls.

Environmental/Ecological Risk: The potential for adverse effects on living organisms associated with pollution of the environment by effluents, emissions, wastes, or accidental chemical releases; energy use; or the depletion of natural resources.

Environmental Equity/Justice: Equal protection from environmental hazards for individuals, groups, or communities regardless of race, ethnicity, or economic status. This applies to the development, implementation, and enforcement of environmental laws, regulations, and policies, and implies that no population of people should be forced to shoulder a disproportionate share of negative environmental impacts of pollution or environmental hazard due to a lack of political or economic strength levels.

Environmental Exposure: Human exposure to pollutants originating from facility emissions. Threshold levels are not necessarily surpassed, but low-level chronic pollutant exposure is one of the most common forms of environmental exposure (See: threshold level).

Environmental Fate: The destiny of a chemical or biological pollutant after release into the environment.

Environmental Fate Data: Data that characterize a pesticide's fate in the ecosystem, considering factors that foster its degradation (light, water, microbes), pathways and resultant products.

Environmental Impact Statement: A document required of federal agencies by the National Environmental Policy Act for major projects or legislative proposals significantly affecting the environment. A tool for decision making, it describes the positive and negative effects of the undertaking and cites alternative actions.

Environmental Indicator: A measurement, statistic or value that provides a proximate gauge or evidence of the effects of environmental management programs or of the state or condition of the environment.

Environmental Justice: The fair treatment of people of all races, cultures, incomes, and educational levels with respect to the development and enforcement of environmental laws, regulations, and policies.

Environmental Lien: A charge, security, or encumbrance on a property's title to secure payment of cost or debt arising from response actions, cleanup, or other remediation of hazardous substances or petroleum products.

Environmental Medium: A major environmental category that surrounds or contacts humans, animals, plants, and other organisms (*e.g.* surface water, ground water, soil or air) and through which chemicals or pollutants move. (See: ambient medium, biological medium.)

Environmental Monitoring for Public Access and Community Tracking: Joint EPA, NOAA, and USGS program to provide timely and effective communication of environmental data and information through improved and updated technology solutions that support timely environmental monitoring reporting, interpreting, and use of the information for the benefit of the public. (See: real-time monitoring.)

Environmental Response Team: EPA experts located in Edison, N.J., and Cincinnati, OH, who can provide around-the-clock technical assistance to EPA regional offices and states during all types of hazardous waste site emergencies and spills of hazardous substances.

Environmental Site Assessment: The process of determining whether contamination is present on a parcel of real property.

Environmental Sustainability: Long-term maintenance of ecosystem components and functions for future generations.

Environmental Tobacco Smoke: Mixture of smoke from the burning end of a cigarette, pipe, or cigar and smoke exhaled by the smoker. (See: passive smoking/secondhand smoke.)

Epidemiology: Study of the distribution of disease, or other health-related states and events in human populations, as related to age, sex, occupation, ethnicity, and economic status in order to identify and alleviate health problems and promote better health.

Epilimnion: Upper waters of a thermally stratified lake subject to wind action.

Episode (Pollution): An air pollution incident in a given area caused by a concentration of atmospheric pollutants under meteorological conditions that may result in a significant increase in illnesses or deaths. May also describe water pollution events or hazardous material spills.

Equilibrium: In relation to radiation, the state at which the radioactivity of consecutive elements within a radioactive series is neither increasing nor decreasing.

Equivalent Method: Any method of sampling and analyzing for air pollution which has been demonstrated to the EPA Administrator's satisfaction to be, under specific conditions, an acceptable alternative to normally used reference methods.

Erosion: The wearing away of land surface by wind or water, intensified by land-clearing practices related to farming, residential or industrial development, road building, or logging.

Established Treatment Technologies: Technologies for which cost and performance data are readily available. (See: Innovative treatment technologies.)

Estimated Environmental Concentration: The estimated pesticide concentration in an ecosystem.

Estuary: Region of interaction between rivers and near-shore ocean waters, where tidal action and river flow mix fresh and salt water. Such areas include bays, mouths of rivers, salt marshes, and lagoons. These brackish water ecosystems shelter and feed marine life, birds, and wildlife. (See: wetlands.)

Ethanol: An alternative automotive fuel derived from grain and corn; usually blended with gasoline to form gasohol.

Ethylene Dibromide (EDB): A chemical used as an agricultural fumigant and in certain industrial processes. Extremely toxic and found to be a carcinogen in laboratory animals, EDB has been banned for most agricultural uses in the United States.

Eutrophic Lakes: Shallow, murky bodies of water with concentrations of plant nutrients causing excessive production of algae. (See: dystrophic lakes.)

Eutrophication: The slow aging process during which a lake, estuary, or bay evolves into a bog or marsh and eventually disappears. During the later stages of eutrophication the water body is choked by abundant plant life due to higher levels of nutritive compounds such as nitrogen and phosphorus. Human activities can accelerate the process.

Evaporation Ponds: Areas where sewage sludge is dumped and dried.

Evapotranspiration: The loss of water from the soil both by evaporation and by transpiration from the plants growing in the soil.

Exceedance: Violation of the pollutant levels permitted by environmental protection standards.

Exclusion: In the asbestos program, one of several situations that permit a Local Education Agency (LEA) to delete one or more of the items required by the Asbestos Hazard Emergency Response Act (AHERA); *e.g.* records of previous asbestos sample collection and analysis may be used by the accredited inspector in lieu of AHERA bulk sampling.

Exclusionary Ordinance: Zoning that excludes classes of persons or businesses from a particular neighborhood or area.

Exempt Solvent: Specific organic compounds not subject to requirements of regulation because they are deemed by EPA to be of negligible photochemical reactivity.

Exempted Aquifer: Underground bodies of water defined in the Underground Injection Control program as aquifers that are potential sources of drinking water though not being used as such, and thus exempted from regulations barring underground injection activities.

Exemption: A state (with primacy) may exempt a public water system from a requirement involving a Maximum Contaminant Level (MCL), treatment technique, or both, if the system cannot comply due to compelling economic or other factors, or because the system was in operation before the requirement or MCL was instituted; and the exemption will not create a public health risk. (See: variance.)

Exotic Species: A species that is not indigenous to a region.

Experimental Use Permit: Obtained by manufacturers for testing new pesticides or uses thereof whenever they conduct experimental field studies to support registration on 10 acres or more of land or one acre or more of water.

Experimental Use Permit: A permit granted by EPA that allows a producer to conduct tests of a new pesticide, product and/or use outside the laboratory. The testing is usually done on ten or more acres of land or water surface.

Explosive Limits: The amounts of vapor in the air that form explosive mixtures; limits are expressed as lower and upper limits and give the range of vapor concentrations in air that will explode if an ignition source is present.

Exports: In solid waste program, municipal solid waste and recyclables transported outside the state or locality where they originated.

Exposure: The amount of radiation or pollutant present in a given environment that represents a potential health threat to living organisms.

Exposure Assessment: Identifying the pathways by which toxicants may reach individuals, estimating how much of a chemical an individual is likely to be exposed to, and estimating the number likely to be exposed.

Exposure Concentration: The concentration of a chemical or other pollutant representing a health threat in a given environment.

Exposure Indicator: A characteristic of the environment measured to provide evidence of the occurrence or magnitude of a response indicator's exposure to a chemical or biological stress.

Exposure Level: The amount (concentration) of a chemical at the absorptive surfaces of an organism.

Exposure Pathway: The path from sources of pollutants via, soil, water, or food to man and other species or settings.

Exposure Route: The way a chemical or pollutant enters an organism after contact; *i.e.* by ingestion, inhalation, or dermal absorption.

Exposure-Response Relationship: The relationship between exposure level and the incidence of adverse effects.

Extraction Procedure (EP Toxic): Determining toxicity by a procedure which simulates leaching; if a certain concentration of a toxic substance can be leached from a waste, that waste is considered hazardous, *i.e.*"EP Toxic."

Extraction Well: A discharge well used to remove groundwater or air.

Extremely Hazardous Substances: Any of 406 chemicals identified by EPA as toxic, and listed under SARA Title III. The list is subject to periodic revision.

F

Fabric Filter: A cloth device that catches dust particles from industrial emissions.

Facilities Plans: Plans and studies related to the construction of treatment works necessary to comply with the Clean Water Act or RCRA. A facilities plan investigates needs and provides information on the cost-effectiveness of alternatives, a recommended plan, an environmental assessment of the recommendations, and descriptions of the treatment works, costs, and a completion schedule.

Facility Emergency Coordinator: Representative of a facility covered by environmental law (e.g, a chemical plant) who participates in the emergency reporting process with the Local Emergency Planning Committee (LEPC).

Facultative Bacteria: Bacteria that can live under aerobic or anaerobic conditions.

Feasibility Study: 1. Analysis of the practicability of a proposal; *e.g.*, a description and analysis of potential cleanup alternatives for a site such as one on the National Priorities List. The feasibility study usually recommends selection of a cost-effective alternative. It usually starts as soon as the remedial investigation is underway; together, they are commonly referred to as the "RI/FS". 2. A small-scale investigation of a problem to ascertain whether a proposed research approach is likely to provide useful data.

Fecal Coliform Bacteria: Bacteria found in the intestinal tracts of mammals. Their presence in water or sludge is an indicator of pollution and possible contamination by pathogens.

Federal Implementation Plan: Under current law, a federally implemented plan to achieve attainment of air quality standards, used when a state is unable to develop an adequate plan.

Federal Motor Vehicle Control Program: All federal actions aimed at controlling pollution from motor vehicles by such efforts as establishing and enforcing tailpipe and evaporative emission standards for new vehicles, testing methods development, and guidance to states operating inspection and maintenance programs. Federally designated area that is required to meet and maintain federal ambient air quality standards. May include nearby locations in the same state or nearby states that share common air pollution problems.

Feedlot: A confined area for the controlled feeding of animals. Tends to concentrate large amounts of animal waste that cannot be absorbed by the soil and, hence, may be carried to nearby streams or lakes by rainfall runoff.

Fen: A type of wetland that accumulates peat deposits. Fens are less acidic than bogs, deriving most of their water from groundwater rich in calcium and magnesium. (See: wetlands.)

Ferrous Metals: Magnetic metals derived from iron or steel; products made from ferrous metals include appliances, furniture, containers, and packaging like steel drums and barrels. Recycled products include processing tin/steel cans, strapping, and metals from appliances into new products.

FIFRA Pesticide Ingredient: An ingredient of a pesticide that must be registered with EPA under the Federal Insecticide, Fungicide, and Rodenticide Act. Products making pesticide claims must register under FIFRA and may be subject to labeling and use requirements.

Fill: Man-made deposits of natural soils or rock products and waste materials.

Filling: Depositing dirt, mud or other materials into aquatic areas to create more dry land, usually for agricultural or commercial development purposes, often with ruinous ecological consequences.

Filter Strip: Strip or area of vegetation used for removing sediment, organic matter, and other pollutants from runoff and wastewater.

Filtration: A treatment process, under the control of qualified operators, for removing solid (particulate) matter from water by means of porous media such as sand or a man-made filter; often used to remove particles that contain pathogens.

Financial Assurance for Closure: Documentation or proof that an owner or operator of a facility such as a landfill or other waste repository is capable of paying the projected costs of closing the facility and monitoring it afterwards as provided in RCRA regulations.

Finding of No Significant Impact: A document prepared by a federal agency showing why a proposed action would not have a significant impact on the environment and thus would not require preparation of an Environmental Impact Statement. An FNSI is based on the results of an environmental assessment.

Finished Water: Water is "finished" when it has passed through all the processes in a water treatment plant and is ready to be delivered to consumers.

First Draw: The water that comes out when a tap is first opened, likely to have the highest level of lead contamination from plumbing materials.

Fix a Sample: A sample is "fixed" in the field by adding chemicals that prevent water quality indicators of interest in the sample from changing before laboratory measurements are made.

Fixed-Location Monitoring: Sampling of an environmental or ambient medium for pollutant concentration at one location continuously or repeatedly.

Flammable: Any material that ignites easily and will burn rapidly.

Flare: A control device that burns hazardous materials to prevent their release into the environment; may operate continuously or intermittently, usually on top of a stack.

Flash Point: The lowest temperature at which evaporation of a substance produces sufficient vapor to form an ignitable mixture with air.

Floc: A clump of solids formed in sewage by biological or chemical action.

Flocculation: Process by which clumps of solids in water or sewage aggregate through biological or chemical action so they can be separated from water or sewage.

Floodplain: The flat or nearly flat land along a river or stream or in a tidal area that is covered by water during a flood.

Floor Sweep: Capture of heavier-than-air gases that collect at floor level.

Flow Rate: The rate, expressed in gallons -or liters-per-hour, at which a fluid escapes from a hole or fissure in a tank. Such measurements are also made of liquid waste, effluent, and surface water movement.

Flowable: Pesticide and other formulations in which the active ingredients are finely ground insoluble solids suspended in a liquid. They are mixed with water for application.

Flowmeter: A gauge indicating the velocity of wastewater moving through a treatment plant or of any liquid moving through various industrial processes.

Flue Gas: The air coming out of a chimney after combustion in the burner it is venting. It can include nitrogen oxides, carbon oxides, water vapor, sulfur oxides, particles and many chemical pollutants.

Flue Gas Desulfurization: A technology that employs a sorbent, usually lime or limestone, to remove sulfur dioxide from the gases produced by burning fossil fuels. Flue gas desulfurization is current state-of-the art technology for major SO2 emitters, like power plants.

Fluidized: A mass of solid particles that is made to flow like a liquid by injection of water or gas is said to have been fluidized. In water treatment, a bed of filter media is fluidized by backwashing water through the filter.

Fluidized Bed Incinerator: An incinerator that uses a bed of hot sand or other granular material to transfer heat directly to waste. Used mainly for destroying municipal sludge.

Flume: A natural or man-made channel that diverts water.

Fluoridation: The addition of a chemical to increase the concentration of fluoride ions in drinking water to reduce the incidence of tooth decay.

Fluorides: Gaseous, solid, or dissolved compounds containing fluorine that result from industrial processes. Excessive amounts in food can lead to fluorosis.

Fluorocarbons (FCs): Any of a number of organic compounds analogous to hydrocarbons in which one or more hydrogen atoms are replaced by fluorine. Once used in the United States as a propellant for domestic aerosols, they are now found mainly in coolants and some industrial processes. FCs containing chlorine are called chlorofluorocarbons (CFCs). They are believed to be modifying the ozone layer in the stratosphere, thereby allowing more harmful solar radiation to reach the Earth's surface.

Flush: 1. To open a cold-water tap to clear out all the water which may have been sitting for a long time in the pipes. In new homes, to flush a system means to send large volumes of water gushing through the unused pipes to remove loose particles of solder and flux. 2. To force large amounts of water through a system to clean out piping or tubing, and storage or process tanks.

Flux: 1. A flowing or flow. 2. A substance used to help metals fuse together.

Fly Ash: Non-combustible residual particles expelled by flue gas.

Fogging: Applying a pesticide by rapidly heating the liquid chemical so that it forms very fine droplets that resemble smoke or fog. Used to destroy mosquitoes, black flies, and similar pests.

Food Chain: A sequence of organisms, each of which uses the next, lower member of the sequence as a food source.

Food Processing Waste: Food residues produced during agricultural and industrial operations.

Food Waste: Uneaten food and food preparation wastes from residences and commercial establishments such as grocery stores, restaurants, and produce stands, institutional cafeterias and kitchens, and industrial sources like employee lunchrooms.

Food Web: The feeding relationships by which energy and nutrients are transferred from one species to another.

Formaldehyde: A colorless, pungent, and irritating gas, CH20, used chiefly as a disinfectant and preservative and in synthesizing other compounds like resins.

Formulation: The substances comprising all active and inert ingredients in a pesticide.

Fossil Fuel: Fuel derived from ancient organic remains; *e.g.* peat, coal, crude oil, and natural gas.

Fracture: A break in a rock formation due to structural stresses; *e.g.* faults, shears, joints, and planes of fracture cleavage.

Free Product: A petroleum hydrocarbon in the liquid free or non aqueous phase. (See: non-aqueous phase liquid.)

Freeboard: 1. Vertical distance from the normal water surface to the top of a confining wall. 2. Vertical distance from the sand surface to the underside of a trough in a sand filter.

Fresh Water: Water that generally contains less than 1,000 milligrams-per-liter of dissolved solids.

Friable: Capable of being crumbled, pulverized, or reduced to powder by hand pressure.

Friable Asbestos: Any material containing more than one-percent asbestos, and that can be crumbled or reduced to powder by hand pressure. (May include previously non-friable material which becomes broken or damaged by mechanical force.)

Fuel Economy Standard: The Corporate Average Fuel Economy Standard (CAFE) effective in 1978. It enhanced the national fuel conservation effort imposing a miles-per-gallon floor for motor vehicles.

Fuel Efficiency: The proportion of energy released by fuel combustion that is converted into useful energy.

Fuel Switching: 1. A precombustion process whereby a low-sulfur coal is used in place of a higher sulfur coal in a power plant to reduce sulfur dioxide emissions. 2. Illegally using leaded gasoline in a motor vehicle designed to use only unleaded.

Fugitive Emissions: Emissions not caught by a capture system.

Fume: Tiny particles trapped in vapor in a gas stream.

Fumigant: A pesticide vaporized to kill pests. Used in buildings and greenhouses.

Functional Equivalent: Term used to describe EPA's decision-making process and its relationship to the environmental review conducted under the National Environmental Policy Act (NEPA). A review is considered functionally equivalent when it addresses the substantive components of a NEPA review.

Fungicide: Pesticides which are used to control, deter, or destroy fungi.

Fungistat: A chemical that keeps fungi from growing.

Fungus (Fungi): Molds, mildews, yeasts, mushrooms, and puffballs, a group of organisms lacking in chlorophyll (*i.e.* are not photosynthetic) and which are usually non-mobile, filamentous, and multicellular. Some grow in soil, others attach themselves to decaying trees and other plants whence they obtain nutrients. Some are pathogens, others stabilize sewage and digest composted waste.

Furrow Irrigation: Irrigation method in which water travels through the field by means of small channels between each groups of rows.

Future Liability: Refers to potentially responsible parties' obligations to pay for additional response activities beyond those specified in the Record of Decision or Consent Decree.

G

Game Fish: Species like trout, salmon, or bass, caught for sport. Many of them show more sensitivity to environmental change than "rough" fish.

Garbage: Animal and vegetable waste resulting from the handling, storage, sale, preparation, cooking, and serving of foods.

Gas Chromatograph/Mass Spectrometer: Instrument that identifies the molecular composition and concentrations of various chemicals in water and soil samples.

Gasahol: Mixture of gasoline and ethanol derived from fermented agricultural products containing at least nine percent ethanol. Gasohol emissions contain less carbon monoxide than those from gasoline.

Gasification: Conversion of solid material such as coal into a gas for use as a fuel.

Gasoline Volatility: The property of gasoline whereby it evaporates into a vapor. Gasoline vapor is a mixture of volatile organic compounds.

General Permit: A permit applicable to a class or category of dischargers.

General Reporting Facility: A facility having one or more hazardous chemicals above the 10,000 pound threshold for planning quantities. Such facilities must file MSDS and emergency inventory information with the SERC, LEPC, and local fire departments.

Generally Recognized as Safe (GRAS): Designation by the FDA that a chemical or substance (including certain pesticides) added to food is considered safe by experts, and so is exempted from the usual FFDCA food additive tolerance requirements.

Generator: 1. A facility or mobile source that emits pollutants into the air or releases hazardous waste into water or soil. 2. Any person, by site, whose act or process produces regulated medical waste or whose act first causes such waste to become subject to regulation. Where more than one person (*e.g.* doctors with separate medical practices) are located in the same building, each business entity is a separate generator.

Genetic Engineering: A process of inserting new genetic information into existing cells in order to modify a specific organism for the purpose of changing one of its characteristics.

Genotoxic: Damaging to DNA; pertaining to agents known to damage DNA.

Geographic Information System (GIS): A computer system designed for storing, manipulating, analyzing, and displaying data in a geographic context.

Geological Log: A detailed description of all underground features (depth, thickness, type of formation) discovered during the drilling of a well.

Geophysical Log: A record of the structure and composition of the earth encountered when drilling a well or similar type of test hold or boring.

Geothermal/Ground Source Heat Pump: These heat pumps are underground coils to transfer heat from the ground to the inside of a building. (See: heat pump; water source heat pump)

Germicide: Any compound that kills disease-causing microorganisms.

Giardia Lamblia: Protozoan in the feces of humans and animals that can cause severe gastrointestinal ailments. It is a common contaminant of surface waters.

Glass Containers: For recycling purposes, containers like bottles and jars for drinks, food, cosmetics and other products. When being recycled, container glass is generally separated into color categories for conversion into new containers, construction materials or fiberglass insulation.

Global Warming: An increase in the near surface temperature of the Earth. Global warming has occurred in the distant past as the result of natural influences, but the term is most often used to refer to the warming predicted to occur as a result of increased emissions of greenhouse gases. Scientists generally agree that the Earth's surface has warmed by about 1 degree Fahrenheit in the past 140 years. The Intergovernmental Panel on Climate Change (IPCC) recently concluded that increased concentrations of greenhouse gases are causing an increase in the Earth's surface temperature and that increased concentrations of sulfate aerosols have led to relative cooling in some regions, generally over and downwind of heavily industrialized areas. (See: climate change)

Global Warming Potential: The ratio of the warming caused by a substance to the warming caused by a similar mass of carbon dioxide. CFC-12, for example, has a GWP of 8,500, while water has a GWP of zero. (See: Class I Substance and Class II Substance.)

Glovebag: A polyethylene or polyvinyl chloride bag-like enclosure affixed around an asbestos containing source (most often thermal system insulation) permitting the material to be removed while minimizing release of airborne fibers to the surrounding atmosphere.

Gooseneck: A portion of a water service connection between the distribution system water main and a meter. Sometimes called a pigtail.

Grab Sample: A single sample collected at a particular time and place that represents the composition of the water, air, or soil only at that time and place.

Grain Loading: The rate at which particles are emitted from a pollution source. Measurement is made by the number of grains per cubic foot of gas emitted.

Granular Activated Carbon Treatment: A filtering system often used in small water systems and individual homes to remove organics. Also used by municipal water treatment plantsd. GAC can be highly effective in lowering elevated levels of radon in water.

Grasscycling: Source reduction activities in which grass clippings are left on the lawn after mowing.

Grassed Waterway: Natural or constructed watercourse or outlet that is shaped or graded and established in suitable vegetation for the disposal of runoff water without erosion.

Gray Water: Domestic wastewater composed of wash water from kitchen, bathroom, and laundry sinks, tubs, and washers.

Greenhouse Effect: The warming of the Earth's atmosphere attributed to a buildup of carbon dioxide or other gases; some scientists think that this build-up allows the sun's rays to heat the Earth, while making the infra-red radiation atmosphere opaque to infra-red radiation, thereby preventing a counterbalancing loss of heat.

Greenhouse Gas: A gas, such as carbon dioxide or methane, which contributes to potential climate change.

Grinder Pump: A mechanical device that shreds solids and raises sewage to a higher elevation through pressure sewers.

Gross Alpha/Beta Particle Activity: The total radioactivity due to alpha or beta particle emissions as inferred from measurements on a dry sample.

Gross Power-Generation Potential: The installed power generation capacity that landfill gas can support.

Ground Cover: Plants grown to keep soil from eroding.

Ground Water: The supply of fresh water found beneath the Earth's surface, usually in aquifers, which supply wells and springs. Because ground water is a major source of drinking water, there is growing concern over contamination from leaching agricultural or industrial pollutants or leaking underground storage tanks.

Ground Water Under the Direct Influence (UDI) of Surface Water: Any water beneath the surface of the ground with: 1. significant occurence of insects or other microorganisms, algae, or large-diameter pathogens; 2. significant and relatively rapid shifts in water characteristics such as turbidity, temperature, conductivity, or pH which closely correlate to climatological or surface water conditions. Direct influence is determined for individual sources in accordance with criteria established by a state.

Ground-Penetrating Radar: A geophysical method that uses high frequency electromagnetic waves to obtain subsurface information.

Ground-Water Discharge: Ground water entering near coastal waters which has been contaminated by landfill leachate, deep well injection of hazardous wastes, septic tanks, etc.

Ground-Water Disinfection Rule: A 1996 amendment of the Safe Drinking Water Act requiring EPA to promulgate national primary drinking water regulations requiring disinfection as for all public water systems, including surface waters and ground water systems.

Gully Erosion: Severe erosion in which trenches are cut to a depth greater than 30 centimeters (a foot). Generally, ditches deep enough to cross with farm equipment are considered gullies.

H

Habitat: The place where a population (*e.g.* human, animal, plant, microorganism) lives and its surroundings, both living and non-living.

Habitat Indicator: A physical attribute of the environment measured to characterize conditions necessary to support an organism, population, or community in the absence of pollutants; *e.g.* salinity of estuarine waters or substrate type in streams or lakes.

Half-Life: 1. The time required for a pollutant to lose one-half of its original coconcentrationor example, the biochemical half-life of DDT in the environment is 15 years. 2. The time required for half of the atoms of a radioactive element to undergo self-transmutation or decay (half-life of radium is 1620 years). 3. The time required for the elimination of half a total dose from the body.

Halogen: A type of incandescent lamp with higher energy-efficiency that standard ones.

Halon: Bromine-containing compounds with long atmospheric lifetimes whose breakdown in the stratosphere causes depletion of ozone. Halons are used in firefighting.

Hammer Mill: A high-speed machine that uses hammers and cutters to crush, grind, chip, or shred solid waste.

Hard Water: Alkaline water containing dissolved salts that interfere with some industrial processes and prevent soap from sudsing.

Hauler: Garbage collection company that offers complete refuse removal service; many will also collect recyclables.

Hazard: 1. Potential for radiation, a chemical or other pollutant to cause human illness or injury. 2. In the pesticide program, the inherent toxicity of a compound. Hazard identification of a given substances is an informed judgment based on verifiable toxicity data from animal models or human studies.

Hazard Assessment: Evaluating the effects of a stressor or determining a margin of safety for an organism by comparing the concentration which causes toxic effects with an estimate of exposure to the organism.

Hazard Communication Standard: An OSHA regulation that requires chemical manufacturers, suppliers, and importers to assess the hazards of the chemicals that they make, supply, or import, and to inform employers, customers, and workers of these hazards through MSDS information.

Hazard Evaluation: A component of risk evaluation that involves gathering and evaluating data on the types of health injuries or diseases that may be produced by a chemical and on the conditions of exposure under which such health effects are produced.

Hazard Identification: Determining if a chemical or a microbe can cause adverse health effects in humans and what those effects might be.

Hazard Quotient: The ratio of estimated site-specific exposure to a single chemical from a site over a specified period to the estimated daily exposure level, at which no adverse health effects are likely to occur.

Hazard Ratio: A term used to compare an animal's daily dietary intake of a pesticide to its LD 50 value. A ratio greater than 1.0 indicates that the animal is likely to consume an a dose amount which would kill 50 percent of animals of the same species. (See: LD 50 /Lethal Dose.)

Hazardous Air Pollutants: Air pollutants which are not covered by ambient air quality standards but which, as defined in the Clean Air Act, may present a threat of adverse human health effects or adverse environmental effects. Such pollutants include asbestos, beryllium, mercury, benzene, coke oven emissions, radionuclides, and vinyl chloride.

Hazardous Chemical: An EPA designation for any hazardous material requiring an MSDS under OSHA's Hazard Communication Standard. Such substances are capable of producing fires and explosions or adverse health effects like cancer and dermatitis. Hazardous chemicals are distinct from hazardous waste.(See: Hazardous Waste.)

Hazardous Ranking System: The principal screening tool used by EPA to evaluate risks to public health and the environment associated with abandoned or uncontrolled hazardous waste sites. The HRS calculates a score based on the potential of hazardous substances spreading from the site through the air, surface water, or ground water, and on other factors such as density and proximity of human population. This score is the primary factor in deciding if the site should be on the National Priorities List and, if so, what ranking it should have compared to other sites on the list.

Hazardous Substance: 1. Any material that poses a threat to human health and/or the environment. Typical hazardous substances are toxic, corrosive, ignitable, explosive, or chemically reactive. 2. Any substance designated by EPA to be reported if a designated quantity of the substance is spilled in the waters of the United States or is otherwise released into the environment.

Hazardous Waste: By-products of society that can pose a substantial or potential hazard to human health or the environment when improperly managed. Possesses at least one of four characteristics (ignitability, corrosivity, reactivity, or toxicity), or appears on special EPA lists.

Hazardous Waste Landfill: An excavated or engineered site where hazardous waste is deposited and covered.

Hazardous Waste Minimization: Reducing the amount of toxicity or waste produced by a facility via source reduction or environmentally sound recycling.

Hazards Analysis: Procedures used to (1) identify potential sources of release of hazardous materials from fixed facilities or transportation accidents; (2) determine the vulnerability of a geographical area to a release of hazardous materials; and (3) compare hazards to determine which present greater or lesser risks to a community.

Hazards Identification: Providing information on which facilities have extremely hazardous substances, what those chemicals are, how much there is at each facility, how the chemicals are stored, and whether they are used at high temperatures.

Headspace: The vapor mixture trapped above a solid or liquid in a sealed vessel.

Health Advisory Level: A non-regulatory health-based reference level of chemical traces (usually in ppm) in drinking water at which there are no adverse health risks when ingested over various periods of time. Such levels are established for one day, 10 days, long-term and life-time exposure periods. They contain a wide margin of safety.

Health Assessment: An evaluation of available data on existing or potential risks to human health posed by a Superfund site. The Agency for Toxic Substances and Disease Registry (ATSDR) of the Department of Health and Human Services (DHHS) is required to perform such an assessment at every site on the National Priorities List.

Heat Island Effect: A "dome" of elevated temperatures over an urban area caused by structural and pavement heat fluxes, and pollutant emissions.

Heat Pump: An electric device with both heating and cooling capabilities. It extracts heat from one medium at a lower (the heat source) temperature and transfers it to another at a higher temperature (the heat sink), thereby cooling the first and warming the second. (See: geothermal, water source heat pump.)

Heavy Metals: Metallic elements with high atomic weights; (*e.g.* mercury, chromium, cadmium, arsenic, and lead); can damage living things at low concentrations and tend to accumulate in the food chain.

Heptachlor: An insecticide that was banned on some food products in 1975 and in all of them 1978. It was allowed for use in seed treatment until 1983. More recently it was found in milk and other dairy products in Arkansas and Missouri where dairy cattle were illegally fed treated seed.

Herbicide: A chemical pesticide designed to control or destroy plants, weeds, or grasses.

Herbivore: An animal that feeds on plants.

Heterotrophic Organisms: Species that are dependent on organic matter for food.

High End Exposure (dose) Estimate: An estimate of exposure, or dose level received anyone in a defined population that is greater than the 90th percentile of all individuals in that population, but less than the exposure at the highest percentile in that population. A high end risk descriptor is an estimate of the risk level for such individuals. Note that risk is based on a combination of exposure and susceptibility to the stressor.

High Intensity Discharge: A generic term for mercury vapor, metal halide, and high pressure sodium lamps and fixtures.

High-Density Polyethylene: A material used to make plastic bottles and other products that produces toxic fumes when burned.

High-Level Nuclear Waste Facility: Plant designed to handle disposal of used nuclear fuel, high level radioactive waste, and plutonium waste.

High-Level Radioactive Waste (HLRW): Waste generated in core fuel of a nuclear reactor, found at nuclear reactors or by nuclear fuel reprocessing; is a serious threat to anyone who comes near the waste without shielding. (See: low-level radioactive waste.)

High-Line Jumpers: Pipes or hoses connected to fire hydrants and laid on top of the ground to provide emergency water service for an isolated portion of a distribution system.

High-Risk Community: A community located within the vicinity of numerous sites of facilities or other potential sources of environmental exposure/health hazards which may result in high levels of exposure to contaminants or pollutants.

High-to-Low-Dose Extrapolation: The process of prediction of low exposure risk to humans and animals from the measured high-exposure-high-risk data involving laboratory animals.

Highest Dose Tested: The highest dose of a chemical or substance tested in a study.

Holding Pond: A pond or reservoir, usually made of earth, built to store polluted runoff.

Holding Time: The maximum amount of time a sample may be stored before analysis.

Hollow Stem Auger Drilling: Conventional drilling method that uses augurs to penetrate the soil. As the augers are rotated, soil cuttings are conveyed to the ground surface via augur spirals. DP tools can be used inside the hollow augers.

Homeowner Water System: Any water system which supplies piped water to a single residence.

Homogeneous Area: In accordance with Asbestos Hazard and Emergency Response Act (AHERA) definitions, an area of surfacing materials, thermal surface insulation, or miscellaneous material that is uniform in color and texture.

Hood Capture Efficiency: Ratio of the emissions captured by a hood and directed into a control or disposal device, expressed as a percent of all emissions.

Host: 1. In genetics, the organism, typically a bacterium, into which a gene from another organism is transplanted. 2. In medicine, an animal infected or parasitized by another organism.

Household Hazardous Waste: Hazardous products used and disposed of by residential as opposed to industrial consumers. Includes paints, stains, varnishes, solvents, pesticides, and other materials or products containing volatile chemicals that can catch fire, react or explode, or that are corrosive or toxic.

Household Waste (Domestic Waste): Solid waste, composed of garbage and rubbish, which normally originates in a private home or apartment house. Domestic waste may contain a significant amount of toxic or hazardous waste.

Human Equivalent Dose: A dose which, when administered to humans, produces an effect equal to that produced by a dose in animals.

Human Exposure Evaluation: Describing the nature and size of the population exposed to a substance and the magnitude and duration of their exposure.

Human Health Risk: The likelihood that a given exposure or series of exposures may have damaged or will damage the health of individuals.

Hydraulic Conductivity: The rate at which water can move through a permeable medium. (*i.e.* the coefficient of permeability.)

Hydraulic Gradient: In general, the direction of groundwater flow due to changes in the depth of the water table.

Hydrocarbons (HC): Chemical compounds that consist entirely of carbon and hydrogen.

Hydrogen Sulfide (H2S): Gas emitted during organic decomposition. Also a by-product of oil refining and burning. Smells like rotten eggs and, in heavy concentration, can kill or cause illness.

Hydrogeological Cycle: The natural process recycling water from the atmosphere down to (and through) the earth and back to the atmosphere again.

Hydrogeology: The geology of ground water, with particular emphasis on the chemistry and movement of water.

Hydrologic Cycle: Movement or exchange of water between the atmosphere and earth.

Hydrology: The science dealing with the properties, distribution, and circulation of water.

Hydrolysis: The decomposition of organic compounds by interaction with water.

Hydronic: A ventilation system using heated or cooled water pumped through a building.

Hydrophilic: Having a strong affinity for water.

Hydrophobic: Having a strong aversion for water.

Hydropneumatic: A water system, usually small, in which a water pump is automatically controlled by the pressure in a compressed air tank.

Hypersensitivity Diseases: Diseases characterized by allergic responses to pollutants; diseases most clearly associated with indoor air quality are asthma, rhinitis, and pneumonic hypersensitivity.

Hypolimnion: Bottom waters of a thermally stratified lake. The hypolimnion of a eutrophic lake is usually low or lacking in oxygen.

Hypoxia/Hypoxic Waters: Waters with dissolved oxygen concentrations of less than 2 ppm, the level generally accepted as the minimum required for most marine life to survive and reproduce.

I

Identification Code or EPA I.D. Number: The unique code assigned to each generator, transporter, and treatment, storage, or disposal facility by regulating agencies to facilitate identification and tracking of chemicals or hazardous waste.

Ignitable: Capable of burning or causing a fire.

IM240: A high-tech, transient dynamometer automobile emissions test that takes up to 240 seconds.

Imhoff Cone: A clear, cone-shaped container used to measure the volume of settleable solids in a specific volume of water.

Immediately Dangerous to Life and Health (IDLH): The maximum level to which a healthy individual can be exposed to a chemical for 30 minutes and escape without suffering irreversible health effects or impairing symptoms. Used as a "level of concern." (See: level of concern.)

Imminent Hazard: One that would likely result in unreasonable adverse effects on humans or the environment or risk unreasonable hazard to an endangered species during the time required for a pesticide registration cancellation proceeding.

Imminent Threat: A high probability that exposure is occurring.

Immiscibility: The inability of two or more substances or liquids to readily dissolve into one another, such as soil and water. Immiscibility The inability of two or more substances or liquids to readily dissolve into one another, such as soil and water.

Impermeable: Not easily penetrated. The property of a material or soil that does not allow, or allows only with great difficulty, the movement or passage of water.

Imports: Municipal solid waste and recyclables that have been transported to a state or locality for processing or final disposition (but that did not originate in that state or locality).

Impoundment: A body of water or sludge confined by a dam, dike, floodgate, or other barrier.

In Situ: In its original place; unmoved unexcavated; remaining at the site or in the subsurface.

In-Line Filtration: Pre-treattment method in which chemicals are mixed by the flowing water; commonly used in pressure filtration installations. Eliminates need for flocculation and sedimentation.

In-Situ Flushing: Introduction of large volumes of water, at times supplemented with cleaning compounds, into soil, waste, or ground water to flush hazardous contaminants from a site.

In-Situ Oxidation: Technology that oxidizes contaminants dissolved in ground water, converting them into insoluble compounds.

In-Situ Stripping: Treatment system that removes or "strips" volatile organic compounds from contaminated ground or surface water by forcing an airstream through the water and causing the compounds to evaporate.

In-Situ Vitrification: Technology that treats contaminated soil in place at extremely high temperatures, at or more than 3000 degrees Fahrenheit.

In Vitro: Testing or action outside an organism (*e.g.* inside a test tube or culture dish.)

In Vivo: Testing or action inside an organism.

Incident Command Post: A facility located at a safe distance from an emergency site, where the incident commander, key staff, and technical representatives can make decisions and deploy emergency manpower and equipment.

Incident Command System (ICS): The organizational arrangement wherein one person, normally the Fire Chief of the impacted district, is in charge of an integrated, comprehensive emergency response organization and the emergency incident site, backed by an Emergency Operations Center staff with resources, information, and advice.

Incineration: A treatment technology involving destruction of waste by controlled burning at high temperatures; *e.g.*, burning sludge to remove the water and reduce the remaining residues to a safe, non-burnable ash that can be disposed of safely on land, in some waters, or in underground locations.

Incineration at Sea: Disposal of waste by burning at sea on specially-designed incinerator ships.

Incinerator: A furnace for burning waste under controlled conditions.

Incompatible Waste: A waste unsuitable for mixing with another waste or material because it may react to form a hazard.

Indemnification: In the pesticide program, legal requirement that EPA pay certain end-users, dealers, and distributors for the cost of stock on hand at the time a pesticide registration is suspended.

Indicator: In biology, any biological entity or processes, or community whose characteristics show the presence of specific environmental conditions. 2. In chemistry, a substance that shows a visible change, usually of color, at a desired point in a chemical reaction. 3.A device that indicates the result of a measurement; *e.g.* a pressure gauge or a moveable scale.

Indirect Discharge: Introduction of pollutants from a non-domestic source into a publicly owned waste-treatment system. Indirect dischargers can be commercial or industrial facilities whose wastes enter local sewers.

Indirect Source: Any facility or building, property, road or parking area that attracts motor vehicle traffic and, indirectly, causes pollution.

Indoor Air: The breathable air inside a habitable structure or conveyance.

Indoor Air Pollution: Chemical, physical, or biological contaminants in indoor air.

Indoor Climate: Temperature, humidity, lighting, air flow and noise levels in a habitable structure or conveyance. Indoor climate can affect indoor air pollution.

Industrial Pollution Prevention: Combination of industrial source reduction and toxic chemical use substitution.

Industrial Process Waste: Residues produced during manufacturing operations.

Industrial Sludge: Semi-liquid residue or slurry remaining from treatment of industrial water and wastewater.

Industrial Source Reduction: Practices that reduce the amount of any hazardous substance, pollutant, or contaminant entering any waste stream or otherwise released into the environment. Also reduces the threat to public health and the environment associated with such releases. Term includes equipment or technology modifications, substitution of raw materials, and improvements in housekeeping, maintenance, training or inventory control.

Industrial Waste: Unwanted materials from an industrial operation; may be liquid, sludge, solid, or hazardous waste.

Inert Ingredient: Pesticide components such as solvents, carriers, dispersants, and surfactants that are not active against target pests. Not all inert ingredients are innocuous.

Inertial Separator: A device that uses centrifugal force to separate waste particles.

Infectious Agent: Any organism, such as a pathogenic virus, parasite, or or bacterium, that is capable of invading body tissues, multiplying, and causing disease.

Infectious Waste: Hazardous waste capable of causing infections in humans, including: contaminated animal waste; human blood and blood products; isolation waste, pathological waste; and discarded sharps (needles, scalpels or broken medical instruments).

Infiltration: 1. The penetration of water through the ground surface into sub-surface soil or the penetration of water from the soil into sewer or other pipes through defective joints, connections, or manhole walls. 2. The technique of applying large volumes of waste water to land to penetrate the surface and percolate through the underlying soil. (See: percolation.)

Infiltration Gallery: A sub-surface groundwater collection system, typically shallow in depth, constructed with open-jointed or perforated pipes that discharge collected water into a watertight chamber from which the water is pumped to treatment facilities and into the distribution system. Usually located close to streams or ponds.

Infiltration Rate: The quantity of water that can enter the soil in a specified time interval.

Inflow: Entry of extraneous rain water into a sewer system from sources other than infiltration, such as basement drains, manholes, storm drains, and street washing.

Influent: Water, wastewater, or other liquid flowing into a reservoir, basin, or treatment plant.

Information Collection Request (ICR): A description of information to be gathered in connection with rules, proposed rules, surveys, and guidance documents that contain information-gathering requirements. The ICR describes what information is needed, why it is needed, how it will be collected, and how much collecting it will cost. The ICR is submitted by the EPA to the Office of Management and Budget (OMB) for approval.

Information File: In the Superfund program, a file that contains accurate, up-to-date documents on a Superfund site. The file is usually located in a public building (school, library, or city hall) convenient for local residents.

Inhalable Particles: All dust capable of entering the human respiratory tract.

Initial Compliance Period (Water): The first full three-year compliance period which begins at least 18 months after promulgation.

Injection Well: A well into which fluids are injected for purposes such as waste disposal, improving the recovery of crude oil, or solution mining.

Injection Zone: A geological formation receiving fluids through a well.

Innovative Technologies: New or inventive methods to treat effectively hazardous waste and reduce risks to human health and the environment.

Innovative Treatment Technologies: Technologies whose routine use is inhibited by lack of data on performance and cost. (See: Established treatment technologies.)

Inoculum: 1. Bacteria or fungi injected into compost to start biological action. 2. A medium containing organisms, usually bacteria or a virus, that is introduced into cultures or living organisms.

Inorganic Chemicals: Chemical substances of mineral origin, not of basically carbon structure.

Insecticide: A pesticide compound specifically used to kill or prevent the growth of insects.

Inspection and Maintenance (I/M): 1. Activities to ensure that vehicles' emission controls work properly. 2. Also applies to wastewater treatment plants and other anti-pollution facilities and processes.

Institutional Waste: Waste generated at institutions such as schools, libraries, hospitals, prisons, etc.

Instream Use: Water use taking place within a stream channel; *e.g.*, hydro-electric power generation, navigation, water quality improvement, fish propagation, recreation.

Integrated Exposure Assessment: Cumulative summation (over time) of the magnitude of exposure to a toxic chemical in all media.

Integrated Pest Management (IPM): A mixture of chemical and other, non-pesticide, methods to control pests.

Integrated Waste Management: Using a variety of practices to handle municipal solid waste; can include source reduction, recycling, incineration, and landfilling.

Interceptor Sewers: Large sewer lines that, in a combined system, control the flow of sewage to the treatment plant. In a storm, they allow some of the sewage to flow directly into a receiving stream, thus keeping it from overflowing onto the streets. Also used in separate systems to collect the flows from main and trunk sewers and carry them to treatment points.

Interface: The common boundary between two substances such as a water and a solid, water and a gas, or two liquids such as water and oil.

Interfacial Tension: The strength of the film separating two immiscible fluids (*e.g.* oil and water) measured in dynes per, or millidynes per centimeter.

Interim (Permit) Status: Period during which treatment, storage and disposal facilities coming under RCRA in 1980 are temporarily permitted to operate while awaiting a permanent permit. Permits issued under these circumstances are usually called "Part A" or "Part B" permits.

Internal Dose: In exposure assessment, the amount of a substance penetrating the absorption barriers (*e.g.* skin, lung tissue, gastrointestinal tract) of an organism through either physical or biological processes. (See: absorbed dose)

Interstate Carrier Water Supply: A source of water for drinking and sanitary use on planes, buses, trains, and ships operating in more than one state. These sources are federally regulated.

Interstate Commerce Clause: A clause of the U.S. Constitution which reserves to the federal government the right to regulate the conduct of business across state lines. Under this clause, for example, the U.S. Supreme Court has ruled that states may not inequitably restrict the disposal of out-of-state wastes in their jurisdictions.

Interstate Waters: Waters that flow across or form part of state or international boundaries; *e.g.* the Great Lakes, the Mississippi River, or coastal waters.

Interstitial Monitoring: The continuous surveillance of the space between the walls of an underground storage tank.

Intrastate Product: Pesticide products once registered by states for sale and use only in the state. All intrastate products have been converted to full federal registration or canceled.

Inventory (TSCA): Inventory of chemicals produced pursuant to Section 8 (b) of the Toxic Substances Control Act.

Inversion: A layer of warm air that prevents the rise of cooling air and traps pollutants beneath it; can cause an air pollution episode.

Ion: An electrically charged atom or group of atoms.

Ion Exchange Treatment: A common water-softening method often found on a large scale at water purification plants that remove some organics and radium by adding calcium oxide or calcium hydroxide to increase the pH to a level where the metals will precipitate out.

Ionization Chamber: A device that measures the intensity of ionizing radiation.

Ionizing Radiation: Radiation that can strip electrons from atoms; *e.g.* alpha, beta, and gamma radiation.

IRIS: EPA's Integrated Risk Information System, an electronic data base containing the Agency's latest descriptive and quantitative regulatory information on chemical constituents.

Irradiated Food: Food subject to brief radioactivity, usually gamma rays, to kill insects, bacteria, and mold, and to permit storage without refrigeration.

Irradiation: Exposure to radiation of wavelengths shorter than those of visible light (gamma, x-ray, or ultra- violet), for medical purposes, to sterilize milk or other foodstuffs, or to induce polymerization of monomers or vulcanization of rubber.

Irreversible Effect: Effect characterized by the inability of the body to partially or fully repair injury caused by a toxic agent.

Irrigation: Applying water or wastewater to land areas to supply the water and nutrient needs of plants.

Irrigation Efficiency: The amount of water stored in the crop root zone compared to the amount of irrigation water applied.

Irrigation Return Flow: Surface and subsurface water which leaves the field following application of irrigation water.

Irritant: A substance that can cause irritation of the skin, eyes, or respiratory system. Effects may be acute from a single high level exposure, or chronic from repeated low-level exposures to such compounds as chlorine, nitrogen dioxide, and nitric acid.

Isoconcentration: More than one sample point exhibiting the same isolate concentration.

Isopleth: The line or area represented by an isoconcentration.

Isotope: A variation of an element that has the same atomic number of protons but a different weight because of the number of neutrons. Various isotopes of the same element may have different radioactive behaviors, some are highly unstable.

Isotropy: The condition in which the hydraulic or other properties of an aquifer are the same in all directions.

J

Jar Test: A laboratory procedure that simulates a water treatment plant's coagulation/flocculation units with differing chemical doses, mix speeds, and settling times to estimate the minimum or ideal coagulant dose required to achieve certain water quality goals.

Joint and Several Liability: Under CERCLA, this legal concept relates to the liability for Superfund site cleanup and other costs on the part of more than one potentially responsible party (*i.e.* if there were several owners or users of a site that became contaminated over the years, they could all be considered potentially liable for cleaning up the site.)

K

Karst: A geologic formation of irregular limestone deposits with sinks, underground streams, and caverns.

Kinetic Energy: Energy possessed by a moving object or water body.

Kinetic Rate Coefficient: A number that describes the rate at which a water constituent such as a biochemical oxygen demand or dissolved oxygen rises or falls, or at which an air pollutant reacts.

L

Laboratory Animal Studies: Investigations using animals as surrogates for humans.

Lagoon: 1. A shallow pond where sunlight, bacterial action, and oxygen work to purify wastewater; also used for storage of wastewater or spent nuclear fuel rods. 2. Shallow body of water, often separated from the sea by coral reefs or sandbars.

Land Application: Discharge of wastewater onto the ground for treatment or reuse. (See: irrigation.)

Land Ban: Phasing out of land disposal of most untreated hazardous wastes, as mandated by the 1984 RCRA amendments.

Land Disposal Restrictions: Rules that require hazardous wastes to be treated before disposal on land to destroy or immobilize hazardous constituents that might migrate into soil and ground water.

Land Farming (of Waste): A disposal process in which hazardous waste deposited on or in the soil is degraded naturally by microbes.

Landfills: 1. Sanitary landfills are disposal sites for non-hazardous solid wastes spread in layers, compacted to the smallest practical volume, and covered by material applied at the end of each operating day. 2. Secure chemical landfills are disposal sites for hazardous waste, selected and designed to minimize the chance of release of hazardous substances into the environment.

Landscape: The traits, patterns, and structure of a specific geographic area, including its biological composition, its physical environment, and its anthropogenic or social patterns. An area where interacting ecosystems are grouped and repeated in similar form.

Landscape Characterization: Documentation of the traits and patterns of the essential elements of the landscape.

Landscape Ecology: The study of the distribution patterns of communities and ecosystems, the ecological processes that affect those patterns, and changes in pattern and process over time.

Landscape Indicator: A measurement of the landscape, calculated from mapped or remotely sensed data, used to describe spatial patterns of land use and land cover across a geographic area. Landscape indicators may be useful as measures of certain kinds of environmental degradation such as forest fragmentation.

Langelier Index (LI): An index reflecting the equilibrium pH of a water with respect to calcium and alkalinity; used in stabilizing water to control both corrosion and scale deposition.

Large Quantity Generator: Person or facility generating more than 2200 pounds of hazardous waste per month. Such generators produce about 90 percent of the nation's hazardous waste, and are subject to all RCRA requirements.

Large Water System: A water system that services more than 50,000 customers.

Laser Induced Fluorescence: A method for measuring the relative amount of soil and/or groundwater with an in-situ sensor.

Latency: Time from the first exposure of a chemical until the appearance of a toxic effect.

Lateral Sewers: Pipes that run under city streets and receive the sewage from homes and businesses, as opposed to domestic feeders and main trunk lines.

Laundering Weir: Sedimention basin overflow weir.

LC 50/Lethal Concentration: Median level concentration, a standard measure of toxicity. It tells how much of a substance is needed to kill half of a group of experimental organisms in a given time. (See: LD 50.)

LD 50/ Lethal Dose: The dose of a toxicant or microbe that will kill 50 percent of the test organisms within a designated period. The lower the LD 50, the more toxic the compound.

Ldlo: Lethal dose low; the lowest dose in an animal study at which lethality occurs.

Leachate: Water that collects contaminants as it trickles through wastes, pesticides or fertilizers. Leaching may occur in farming areas, feedlots, and landfills, and may result in hazardous substances entering surface water, ground water, or soil.

Leachate Collection System: A system that gathers leachate and pumps it to the surface for treatment.

Leaching: The process by which soluble constituents are dissolved and filtered through the soil by a percolating fluid. (See: leachate.)

Lead (Pb): A heavy metal that is hazardous to health if breathed or swallowed. Its use in gasoline, paints, and plumbing compounds has been sharply restricted or eliminated by federal laws and regulations. (See: heavy metals.)

Lead Service Line: A service line made of lead which connects the water to the building inlet and any lead fitting connected to it.

Legionella: A genus of bacteria, some species of which have caused a type of pneumonia called Legionaires Disease.

Lethal Concentration 50: Also referred to as LC50, a concentration of a pollutant or effluent at which 50 percent of the test organisms die; a common measure of acute toxicity.

Lethal Dose 50: Also referred to as LD50, the dose of a toxicant that will kill 50 percent of test organisms within a designated period of time; the lower the LD 50, the more toxic the compound.

Level of Concern (LOC): The concentration in air of an extremely hazardous substance above which there may be serious immediate health effects to anyone exposed to it for short periods

Life Cycle of a Product: All stages of a product's development, from extraction of fuel for power to production, marketing, use, and disposal.

Lifetime Average Daily Dose: Figure for estimating excess lifetime cancer risk.

Lifetime Exposure: Total amount of exposure to a substance that a human would receive in a lifetime (usually assumed to be 70 years).

Lift: In a sanitary landfill, a compacted layer of solid waste and the top layer of cover material.

Lifting Station: (See: pumping station.)

Light Non-Aqueous Phase Liquid (LNAPL): A non-aqueous phase liquid with a specific gravity less than 1.0. Because the specific gravity of water is 1.0, most LNAPLs float on top of the water table. Most common petroleum hydrocarbon fuels and lubricating oils are LNAPLs.

Light-Emitting Diode: A long-lasting illumination technology used for exit signs which requires very little power

Limestone Scrubbing: Use of a limestone and water solution to remove gaseous stack-pipe sulfur before it reaches the atmosphere.

Limit of Detection (LOD): The minimum concentration of a substance being analyzed test that has a 99 percent probability of being identified.

Limited Degradation: An environmental policy permitting some degradation of natural systems but terminating at a level well beneath an established health standard.

Limiting Factor: A condition whose absence or excessive concentration, is incompatible with the needs or tolerance of a species or population and which may have a negative influence on their ability to thrive.

Limnology: The study of the physical, chemical, hydrological, and biological aspects of fresh water bodies.

Lindane: A pesticide that causes adverse health effects in domestic water supplies and is toxic to freshwater fish and aquatic life.

Liner: 1. A relatively impermeable barrier designed to keep leachate inside a landfill. Liner materials include plastic and dense clay. 2. An insert or sleeve for sewer pipes to prevent leakage or infiltration.

Lipid Solubility: The maximum concentration of a chemical that will dissolve in fatty substances. Lipid soluble substances are insoluble in water. They will very selectively disperse through the environment via uptake in living tissue.

Liquefaction: Changing a solid into a liquid.

Liquid Injection Incinerator: Commonly used system that relies on high pressure to prepare liquid wastes for incineration by breaking them up into tiny droplets to allow easier combustion.

List: Shorthand term for EPA list of violating facilities or firms debarred from obtaining government contracts because they violated certain sections of the Clean Air or Clean Water Acts. The list is maintained by The Office of Enforcement and Compliance Monitoring.

Listed Waste: Wastes listed as hazardous under RCRA but which have not been subjected to the Toxic Characteristics Listing Process because the dangers they present are considered self-evident.

Lithology: Mineralogy, grain size, texture, and other physical properties of granular soil, sediment, or rock.

Litter: 1. The highly visible portion of solid waste carelessly discarded outside the regular garbage and trash collection and disposal system. 2. leaves and twigs fallen from forest trees.

Littoral Zone: 1. That portion of a body of fresh water extending from the shoreline lakeward to the limit of occupancy of rooted plants. 2. A strip of land along the shoreline between the high and low water levels.

Local Education Agency (LEA): In the asbestos program, an educational agency at the local level that exists primarily to operate schools or to contract for educational services, including primary and secondary public and private schools. A single, unaffiliated school can be considered an LEA for AHERA purposes.

Local Emergency Planning Committee (LEPC): A committee appointed by the state emergency response commission, as required by SARA Title III, to formulate a comprehensive emergency plan for its jurisdiction.

Low Density Polyethylene (LOPE): Plastic material used for both rigid containers and plastic film applications.

Low Emissivity (low-E) Windows: New window technology that lowers the amount of energy loss through windows by inhibiting the transmission of radiant heat while still allowing sufficient light to pass through.

Low NOx Burners: One of several combustion technologies used to reduce emissions of Nitrogen Oxides (NOx.)

Low-Level Radioactive Waste (LLRW): Wastes less hazardous than most of those associated with a nuclear reactor; generated by hospitals, research laboratories, and certain industries. The Department of Energy, Nuclear Regulatory Commission, and EPA share responsibilities for managing them. (See: high-level radioactive wastes.)

Lower Detection Limit: The smallest signal above background noise an instrument can reliably detect.

Lower Explosive Limit (LEL): The concentration of a compound in air below which the mixture will not catch on fire.

Lowest Acceptable Daily Dose: The largest quantity of a chemical that will not cause a toxic effect, as determined by animal studies.

Lowest Achievable Emission Rate: Under the Clean Air Act, the rate of emissions that reflects the most stringent emission limitation in the implementation plan of any state for such source unless the owner or operator demonstrates such limitations are not achievable; or (2) the most stringent emissions limitation achieved in practice, whichever is more stringent. A proposed new or modified source may not emit pollutants in excess of existing new source standards.

Lowest Observed Adverse Effect Level (LOAEL): The lowest level of a stressor that causes statistically and biologically significant differences in test samples as compared to other samples subjected to no stressor.

M

Macropores: Secondary soil features such as root holes or desiccation cracks that can create significant conduits for movement of NAPL and dissolved contaminants, or vapor-phase contaminants.

Magnetic Separation: Use of magnets to separate ferrous materials from mixed municipal waste stream.

Major Modification: This term is used to define modifications of major stationary sources of emissions with respect to Prevention of Significant Deterioration and New Source Review under the Clean Air Act.

Major Stationary Sources: Term used to determine the applicability of Prevention of Significant Deterioration and new source regulations. In a nonattainment area, any stationary pollutant source with potential to emit more than 100 tons per year is considered a major stationary source. In PSD areas the cutoff level may be either 100 or 250 tons, depending upon the source.

Majors: Larger publicly owned treatment works (POTWs) with flows equal to at least one million gallons per day (mgd) or servicing a population equivalent to 10,000 persons; certain other POTWs having significant water quality impacts. (See: minors.)

Man-Made (Anthropogenic) Beta Particle and Photon Emitters: All radionuclides emitting beta particles and/or photons listed in Maximum Permissible Body Burdens and Maximum Permissible Concentrations of Radonuclides in Air and Water for Occupational Exposure.

Management Plan: Under the Asbestos Hazard Emergency Response Act (AHERA), a document that each Local Education Agency is required to prepare, describing all activities planned and undertaken by a school to comply with AHERA regulations, including building inspections to identify asbestos containing materials, response actions, and operations and maintenance programs to minimize the risk of exposure.

Managerial Controls: Methods of nonpoint source pollution control based on decisions about managing agricultural wastes or application times or rates for agrochemicals.

Mandatory Recycling: Programs which by law require consumers to separate trash so that some or all recyclable materials are recovered for recycling rather than going to landfills.

Manifest: A one-page form used by haulers transporting waste that lists EPA identification numbers, type and quantity of waste, the generator it originated from, the transporter that shipped it, and the storage or disposal facility to which it is being shipped. It includes copies for all participants in the shipping process.

Manifest System: Tracking of hazardous waste from "cradle-to-grave" (generation through disposal) with accompanying documents known as manifests.(See: cradle to grave.)

Manual Separation: Hand sorting of recyclable or compostable materials in waste.

Manufacturer's Formulation: A list of substances or component parts as described by the maker of a coating, pesticide, or other product containing chemicals or other substances.

Manufacturing Use Product: Any product intended (labeled) for formulation or repackaging into other pesticide products.

Margin of Safety: Maximum amount of exposure producing no measurable effect in animals (or studied humans) divided by the actual amount of human exposure in a population.

Margin of Exposure (MOE): The ratio of the no-observed adverse-effect-level to the estimated exposure dose.

Marine Sanitation Device: Any equipment or process installed on board a vessel to receive, retain, treat, or discharge sewage.

Marsh: A type of wetland that does not accumulate appreciable peat deposits and is dominated by herbaceous vegetation. Marshes may be either fresh or saltwater, tidal or non-tidal. (See: wetlands.)

Material Category: In the asbestos program, broad classification of materials into thermal surfacing insulation, surfacing material, and miscellaneous material.

Material Safety Data Sheet (MSDS): A compilation of information required under the OSHA Communication Standard on the identity of hazardous chemicals, health, and physical hazards, exposure limits, and precautions. Section 311 of SARA requires facilities to submit MSDSs under certain circumstances.

Material Type: Classification of suspect material by its specific use or application; *e.g.*, pipe insulation, fireproofing, and floor tile.

Materials Recovery Facility (MRF): A facility that processes residentially collected mixed recyclables into new products available for market.

Maximally (or Most) Exposed Individual: The person with the highest exposure in a given population.

Maximum Acceptable Toxic Concentration: For a given ecological effects test, the range (or geometric mean) between the No Observable Adverse Effect Level and the Lowest Observable Adverse Effects Level.

Maximum Available Control Technology (MACT): The emission standard for sources of air pollution requiring the maximum reduction of hazardous emissions, taking cost and feasibility into account. Under the Clean Air Act Amendments of 1990, the MACT must not be less than the average emission level achieved by controls on the best performing 12 percent of existing sources, by category of industrial and utility sources.

Maximum Contaminant Level: The maximum permissible level of a contaminant in water delivered to any user of a public system. MCLs are enforceable standards.

Maximum Contaminant Level Goal (MCLG): Under the Safe Drinking Water Act, a non-enforceable concentration of a drinking water contaminant, set at the level at which no known or anticipated adverse effects on human health occur and which allows an adequate safety margin. The MCLG is usually the starting point for determining the regulated Maximum Contaminant Level. (See: maximum contaminant level.)

Maximum Exposure Range: Estimate of exposure or dose level received by an individual in a defined population that is greater than the 98th percentile dose for all individuals in that population, but less than the exposure level received by the person receiving the highest exposure level.

Maximum Residue Level: Comparable to a U.S. tolerance level, the Maximum Residue Level the enforceable limit on food pesticide levels in some countries. Levels are set by the Codex Alimentarius Commission, a United Nations agency managed and funded jointly by the World Health Organization and the Food and Agriculture Organization.

Maximum Tolerated Dose: The maximum dose that an animal species can tolerate for a major portion of its lifetime without significant impairment or toxic effect other than carcinogenicity.

Measure of Effect/ Measurement Endpoint: A measurable characteristic of ecological entity that can be related to an assessment endpoint; *e.g.* a laboratory test for eight species meeting certain requirements may serve as a measure of effect for an assessment endpoint, such as survival of fish, aquatic, invertebrate or algal species under acute exposure.

Measure of Exposure: A measurable characteristic of a stressor (such as the specific amount of mercury in a body of water) used to help quantify the exposure of an ecological entity or individual organism.

Mechanical Aeration: Use of mechanical energy to inject air into water to cause a waste stream to absorb oxygen.

Mechanical Separation: Using mechanical means to separate waste into various components.

Mechanical Turbulence: Random irregularities of fluid motion in air caused by buildings or other nonthermal, processes.

Media: Specific environments—air, water, soil—which are the subject of regulatory concern and activities.

Medical Surveillance: A periodic comprehensive review of a worker's health status; acceptable elements of such surveillance program are listed in the Occupational Safety and Health Administration standards for asbestos.

Medical Waste: Any solid waste generated in the diagnosis, treatment, or immunization of human beings or animals, in research pertaining thereto, or in the production or testing of biological, excluding hazardous waste identified or listed under 40 CFR Part 261 or any household waste as defined in 40 CFR Sub-section 261.4 (b)(1).

Medium-size Water System: A water system that serves 3,300 to 50,000 customers.

Meniscus: The curved top of a column of liquid in a small tube.

Mercury (Hg): Heavy metal that can accumulate in the environment and is highly toxic if breathed or swallowed. (See:heavy metals.)

Mesotrophic: Reservoirs and lakes which contain moderate quantities of nutrients and are moderately productive in terms of aquatic animal and plant life.

Metabolites: Any substances produced by biological processes, such as those from pesticides.

Metalimnion: The middle layer of a thermally stratified lake or reservoir. In this layer there is a rapid decrease in temperature with depth. Also called thermocline.

Methane: A colorless, nonpoisonous, flammable gas created by anaerobic decomposition of organic compounds. A major component of natural gas used in the home.

Methanol: An alcohol that can be used as an alternative fuel or as a gasoline additive. It is less volatile than gasoline; when blended with gasoline it lowers the carbon monoxide emissions but increases hydrocarbon emissions. Used as pure fuel, its emissions are less ozone-forming than those from gasoline. Poisonous to humans and animals if ingested.

Method 18: An EPA test method which uses gas chromatographic techniques to measure the concentration of volatile organic compounds in a gas stream.

Method 24: An EPA reference method to determine density, water content and total volatile content (water and VOC) of coatings.

Method 25: An EPA reference method to determine the VOC concentration in a gas stream.

Method Detection Limit (MDL): See limit of detection.

Methoxychlor: Pesticide that causes adverse health effects in domestic water supplies and is toxic to freshwater and marine aquatic life.

Methyl Orange Alkalinity: A measure of the total alkalinity in a water sample in which the color of methyl orange reflects the change in level.

Microbial Growth: The amplification or multiplication of microorganisms such as bacteria, algae, diatoms, plankton, and fungi.

Microbial Pesticide: A microorganism that is used to kill a pest, but is of minimum toxicity to humans.

Microclimate: 1. Localized climate conditions within an urban area or neighborhood. 2. The climate around a tree or shrub or a stand of trees.

Microenvironmental Method: A method for sequentially assessing exposure for a series of microenvironments that can be approximated by constant concentrations of a stressor.

Microenvironments: Well-defined surroundings such as the home, office, or kitchen that can be treated as uniform in terms of stressor concentration.

Million-Gallons Per Day (MGD): A measure of water flow.

Minimization: A comprehensive program to minimize or eliminate wastes, usually applied to wastes at their point of origin. (See: waste minimization.)

Mining of an Aquifer: Withdrawal over a period of time of ground water that exceeds the rate of recharge of the aquifer.

Mining Waste: Residues resulting from the extraction of raw materials from the earth.

Minor Source: New emissions sources or modifications to existing emissions sources that do not exceed NAAQS emission levels.

Minors: Publicly owned treatment works with flows less than 1 million gallons per day. (See: majors.)

Miscellaneous ACM: Interior asbestos-containing building material or structural components, members or fixtures, such as floor and ceiling tiles; does not include surfacing materials or thermal system insulation.

Miscellaneous Materials: Interior building materials on structural components, such as floor or ceiling tiles.

Miscible Liquids: Two or more liquids that can be mixed and will remain mixed under normal conditions.

Missed Detection: The situation that occurs when a test indicates that a tank is "tight" when in fact it is leaking.

Mist: Liquid particles measuring 40 to 500 micrometers (pm), are formed by condensation of vapor. By comparison, fog particles are smaller than 40 micrometers (pm).

Mitigation: Measures taken to reduce adverse impacts on the environment.

Mixed Funding: Settlements in which potentially responsible parties and EPA share the cost of a response action.

Mixed Glass: Recovered container glass not sorted into categories (*e.g.* color, grade).

Mixed Liquor: A mixture of activated sludge and water containing organic matter undergoing activated sludge treatment in an aeration tank.

Mixed Metals: Recovered metals not sorted into categories such as aluminum, tin, or steel cans or ferrous or non-ferrous metals.

Mixed Municipal Waste: Solid waste that has not been sorted into specific categories (such as plastic, glass, yard trimmings, etc.)

Mixed Paper: Recovered paper not sorted into categories such as old magazines, old newspapers, old corrugated boxes, etc.

Mixed Plastic: Recovered plastic unsorted by category.

Mobile Incinerator Systems: Hazardous waste incinerators that can be transported from one site to another.

Mobile Source: Any non-stationary source of air pollution such as cars, trucks, motorcycles, buses, airplanes, and locomotives.

Model Plant: A hypothetical plant design used for developing economic, environmental, and energy impact analyses as support for regulations or regulatory guidelines; first step in exploring the economic impact of a potential NSPS.

Modified Bin Method: Way of calculating the required heating or cooling for a building based on determining how much energy the system would use if outdoor temperatures were within a certain temperature interval and then multiplying the energy use by the time the temperature interval typically occurs.

Modified Source: The enlargement of a major stationary pollutant sources is often referred to as modification, implying that more emissions will occur.

Moisture Content: 1.The amount of water lost from soil upon drying to a constant weight, expressed as the weight per unit of dry soil or as the volume of water per unit bulk volume of the soil. For a fully saturated medium, moisture content indicates the porosity. 2. Water equivalent of snow on the ground; an indicator of snowmelt flood potential.

Molecule: The smallest division of a compound that still retains or exhibits all the properties of the substance.

Molten Salt Reactor: A thermal treatment unit that rapidly heats waste in a heat-conducting fluid bath of carbonate salt.

Monitoring: Periodic or continuous surveillance or testing to determine the level of compliance with statutory requirements and/or pollutant levels in various media or in humans, plants, and animals.

Monitoring Well: 1. A well used to obtain water quality samples or measure groundwater levels. 2. A well drilled at a hazardous waste management facility or Superfund site to collect groundwater samples for the purpose of physical, chemical, or biological analysis to determine the amounts, types, and distribution of contaminants in the groundwater beneath the site.

Monoclonal Antibodies (Also called MABs and MCAs): 1. Man-made (anthropogenic) clones of a molecule, produced in quantity for medical or research purposes. 2. Molecules of living organisms that selectively find and attach to other molecules to which their structure conforms exactly. This could also apply to equivalent activity by chemical molecules.

Monomictic: Lakes and reservoirs which are relatively deep, do not freeze over during winter, and undergo a single stratification and mixing cycle during the year (usually in the fall).

Montreal Protocol: Treaty, signed in 1987, governs stratospheric ozone protection and research, and the production and use of ozone-depleting substances. It provides for the end of production of ozone depleting substances such as CFCS. Under the Protocol, various research groups continue to assess the ozone layer. The Multilateral Fund provides resources to developing nations to promote the transition to ozone-safe technologies.

Moratorium: During the negotiation process, a period of 60 to 90 days during which EPA and potentially responsible parties may reach settlement but no site response activities can be conducted.

Morbidity: Rate of disease incidence.

Mortality: Death rate.

Most Probable Number: An estimate of microbial density per unit volume of water sample, based on probability theory.

Muck Soils: Earth made from decaying plant materials.

Mudballs: Round material that forms in filters and gradually increases in size when not removed by backwashing.

Mulch: A layer of material (wood chips, straw, leaves, etc.) placed around plants to hold moisture, prevent weed growth, and enrich or sterilize the soil.

Multi-Media Approach: Joint approach to several environmental media, such as air, water, and land.

Multiple Chemical Sensitivity: A diagnostic label for people who suffer multi-system illnesses as a result of contact with, or proximity to, a variety of airborne agents and other substances.

Multiple Use: Use of land for more than one purpose; *e.g.*, grazing of livestock, watershed and wildlife protection, recreation, and timber production. Also applies to use of bodies of water for recreational purposes, fishing, and water supply.

Multistage Remote Sensing: A strategy for landscape characterization that involves gathering and analyzing information at several geographic scales, ranging from generalized levels of detail at the national level through high levels of detail at the local scale.

Municipal Discharge: Discharge of effluent from waste water treatment plants which receive waste water from households, commercial establishments, and industries in the coastal drainage basin. Combined sewer/separate storm overflows are included in this category.

Municipal Sewage: Wastes (mostly liquid) originating from a community; may be composed of domestic wastewaters and/or industrial discharges.

Municipal Sludge: Semi-liquid residue remaining from the treatment of municipal water and wastewater.

Municipal Solid Waste: Common garbage or trash generated by industries, businesses, institutions, and homes.

Mutagen/Mutagenicity: An agent that causes a permanent genetic change in a cell other than that which occurs during normal growth. Mutagenicity is the capacity of a chemical or physical agent to cause such permanent changes.

N

National Ambient Air Quality Standards (NAAQS): Standards established by EPA that apply for outdoor air throughout the country. (See: criteria pollutants, state implementation plans, emissions trading.)

National Emissions Standards for Hazardous Air Pollutants (NESHAPS): Emissions standards set by EPA for an air pollutant not covered by NAAQS that may cause an increase in fatalities or in serious, irreversible, or incapacitating illness. Primary standards are designed to protect human health, secondary standards to protect public welfare (*e.g.* building facades, visibility, crops, and domestic animals).

National Environmental Performance Partnership Agreements: System that allows states to assume greater responsibility for environmental programs based on their relative ability to execute them.

National Estuary Program: A program established under the Clean Water Act Amendments of 1987 to develop and implement conservation and management plans for protecting estuaries and restoring and maintaining their chemical, physical, and biological integrity, as well as controlling point and nonpoint pollution sources.

National Municipal Plan: A policy created in 1984 by EPA and the states in 1984 to bring all publicly owned treatment works (POTWs) into compliance with Clean Water Act requirements.

National Oil and Hazardous Substances Contingency Plan (NOHSCP/NCP): The federal regulation that guides determination of the sites to be corrected under both the Superfund program and the program to prevent or control spills into surface waters or elsewhere.

National Pollutant Discharge Elimination System (NPDES): A provision of the Clean Water Act which prohibits discharge of pollutants into waters of the United States unless a special permit is issued by EPA, a state, or, where delegated, a tribal government on an Indian reservation.

National Priorities List (NPL): EPA's list of the most serious uncontrolled or abandoned hazardous waste sites identified for possible long-term remedial action under Superfund. The list is based primarily on the score a site receives from the Hazard Ranking System. EPA is required to update the NPL at least once a year. A site must be on the NPL to receive money from the Trust Fund for remedial action.

National Response Center: The federal operations center that receives notifications of all releases of oil and hazardous substances into the environment; open 24 hours a day, is operated by the U.S. Coast Guard, which evaluates all reports and notifies the appropriate agency.

National Response Team (NRT): Representatives of 13 federal agencies that, as a team, coordinate federal responses to nationally significant incidents of pollution—an oil spill, a major chemical release, or a - superfund response action—and provide advice and technical assistance to the responding agency(ies) before and during a response action.

National Secondary Drinking Water Regulations: Commonly referred to as NSDWRs.

Navigable Waters: Traditionally, waters sufficiently deep and wide for navigation by all, or specified vessels; such waters in the United States come under federal jurisdiction and are protected by certain provisions of the Clean Water Act.

Necrosis: Death of plant or animal cells or tissues. In plants, necrosis can discolor stems or leaves or kill a plant entirely.

Negotiations (Under Superfund): After potentially responsible parties are identified for a site, EPA coordinates with them to reach a settlement that will result in the PRP paying for or conducting the cleanup under EPA supervision. If negotiations fail, EPA can order the PRP to conduct the cleanup or EPA can pay for the cleanup using Superfund monies and then sue to recover the costs.

Nematocide: A chemical agent which is destructive to nematodes.

Nephelometric: Method of of measuring turbidity in a water sample by passing light through the sample and measuring the amount of the light that is deflected.

Netting: A concept in which all emissions sources in the same area that owned or controlled by a single company are treated as one large source, thereby allowing flexibility in controlling individual sources in order to meet a single emissions standard. (See: bubble.)

Neutralization: Decreasing the acidity or alkalinity of a substance by adding alkaline or acidic materials, respectively.

New Source: Any stationary source built or modified after publication of final or proposed regulations that prescribe a given standard of performance.

New Source Performance Standards (NSPS): Uniform national EPA air emission and water effluent standards which limit the amount of pollution allowed from new sources or from modified existing sources.

New Source Review (NSR): A Clean Air Act requirement that State Implementation Plans must include a permit review that applies to the construction and operation of new and modified stationary sources in nonattainment areas to ensure attainment of national ambient air quality standards.

Nitrate: A compound containing nitrogen that can exist in the atmosphere or as a dissolved gas in water and which can have harmful effects on humans and animals. Nitrates in water can cause severe illness in infants and domestic animals. A plant nutrient and inorganic fertilizer, nitrate is found in septic systems, animal feed lots, agricultural fertilizers, manure, industrial waste waters, sanitary landfills, and garbage dumps.

Nitric Oxide (NO): A gas formed by combustion under high temperature and high pressure in an internal combustion engine; it is converted by sunlight and photochemical processes in ambient air to nitrogen oxide. NO is a precursor of ground-level ozone pollution, or smog..

Nitrification: The process whereby ammonia in wastewater is oxidized to nitrite and then to nitrate by bacterial or chemical reactions.

Nitrilotriacetic Acid (NTA): A compound now replacing phosphates in detergents.

Nitrite: 1. An intermediate in the process of nitrification. 2. Nitrous oxide salts used in food preservation.

Nitrogen Dioxide (NO2): The result of nitric oxide combining with oxygen in the atmosphere; major component of photochemical smog.

Nitrogen Oxide (NOx): The result of photochemical reactions of nitric oxide in ambient air; major component of photochemical smog. Product of combustion from transportation and stationary sources and a major contributor to the formation of ozone in the troposphere and to acid deposition.

Nitrogenous Wastes: Animal or vegetable residues that contain significant amounts of nitrogen.

Nitrophenols: Synthetic organopesticides containing carbon, hydrogen, nitrogen, and oxygen.

No Further Remedial Action Planned: Determination made by EPA following a preliminary assessment that a site does not pose a significant risk and so requires no further activity under CERCLA.

No Observable Adverse Effect Level (NOAEL): An exposure level at which there are no statistically or biologically significant increases in the frequency or severity of adverse effects between the exposed population and its appropriate control; some effects may be produced at this level, but they are not considered as adverse, or as precurors to adverse effects. In an experiment with several NOAELs, the regulatory focus is primarily on the highest one, leading to the common usage of the term NOAEL as the highest exposure without adverse effects.

No Till: Planting crops without prior seedbed preparation, into an existing cover crop, sod, or crop residues, and eliminating subsequent tillage operations.

No-Observed-Effect-Level (NOEL): Exposure level at which there are no statistically or biological significant differences in the frequency or severity of any effect in the exposed or control populations.

Noble Metal: Chemically inactive metal such as gold; does not corrode easily.

Noise: Product-level or product-volume changes occurring during a test that are not related to a leak but may be mistaken for one.

Non-Aqueous Phase Liquid (NAPL): Contaminants that remain undiluted as the original bulk liquid in the subsurface, *e.g.* spilled oil. (See: fee product.)

Non-Attainment Area: Area that does not meet one or more of the National Ambient Air Quality Standards for the criteria pollutants designated in the Clean Air Act.

Non-Binding Allocations of Responsibility (NBAR): A process for EPA to propose a way for potentially responsible parties to allocate costs among themselves.

Non-Community Water System: A public water system that is not a community water system; *e.g.* the water supply at a camp site or national park.

Non-Compliance Coal: Any coal that emits greater than 3.0 pounds of sulfur dioxide per million BTU when burned. Also known as high-sulfur coal.

Non-Contact Cooling Water: Water used for cooling which does not come into direct contact with any raw material, product, byproduct, or waste.

Non-Conventional Pollutant: Any pollutant not statutorily listed or which is poorly understood by the scientific community.

Non-Degradation: An environmental policy which disallows any lowering of naturally occurring quality regardless of pre established health standards.

Non-Ferrous Metals: Nonmagnetic metals such as aluminum, lead, and copper. Products made all or in part from such metals include containers, packaging, appliances, furniture, electronic equipment and aluminum foil.

Non-ionizing Electromagnetic Radiation: 1. Radiation that does not change the structure of atoms but does heat tissue and may cause harmful biological effects. 2. Microwaves, radio waves, and low frequency electromagnetic fields from high-voltage transmission lines.

Non-Methane Hydrocarbon (NMHC): The sum of all hydrocarbon air pollutants except methane; significant precursors to ozone formation.

Non-Methane Organic Gases (NMOG): The sum of all organic air pollutants. Excluding methane; they account for aldehydes, ketones, alcohols, and other pollutants that are not hydrocarbons but are precursors of ozone.

Non-Point Sources: Diffuse pollution sources (*i.e.* without a single point of origin or not introduced into a receiving stream from a specific outlet). The pollutants are generally carried off the land by storm water. Common non-point sources are agriculture, forestry, urban, mining, construction, dams, channels, land disposal, saltwater intrusion, and city streets.

Non-potable: Water that is unsafe or unpalatable to drink because it contains pollutants, contaminants, minerals, or infective agents.

Non-Road Emissions: Pollutants emitted by combustion engines on farm and construction equipment, gasoline-powered lawn and garden equipment, and power boats and outboard motors.

Non-Transient Non-Community Water System: A public water system that regularly serves at least 25 of the same non-resident persons per day for more than six months per year.

Nondischarging Treatment Plant: A treatment plant that does not discharge treated wastewater into any stream or river. Most are pond systems that dispose of the total flow they receive by means of evaporation or percolation to groundwater, or facilities that dispose of their effluent by recycling or reuse (*e.g.* spray irrigation or groundwater discharge).

Nonfriable Asbestos-Containing Materials: Any material containing more than one percent asbestos (as determined by Polarized Light Microscopy) that, when dry, cannot be crumbled, pulverized, or reduced to powder by hand pressure.

Nonhazardous Industrial Waste: Industrial process waste in wastewater not considered municipal solid waste or hazardous waste under RARA.

Notice of Deficiency: An EPA request to a facility owner or operator requesting additional information before a preliminary decision on a permit application can be made.

Notice of Intent to Cancel: Notification sent to registrants when EPA decides to cancel registration of a product containing a pesticide.

Notice of Intent to Deny: Notification by EPA of its preliminary intent to deny a permit application.

Notice of Intent to Suspend: Notification sent to a pesticide registrant when EPA decides to suspend product sale and distribution because of failure to submit requested data in a timely and/or acceptable manner, or because of imminent hazard. (See: emergency suspension.)

Nuclear Reactors and Support Facilities: Uranium mills, commercial power reactors, fuel reprocessing plants, and uranium enrichment facilities.

Nuclear Winter: Prediction by some scientists that smoke and debris rising from massive fires of a nuclear war could block sunlight for weeks or months, cooling the earth's surface and producing climate changes that could, for example, negatively affect world agricultural and weather patterns.

Nuclide: An atom characterized by the number of protons, neturons, and energy in the nucleus.

Nutrient: Any substance assimilated by living things that promotes growth. The term is generally applied to nitrogen and phosphorus in wastewater, but is also applied to other essential and trace elements.

Nutrient Pollution: Contamination of water resources by excessive inputs of nutrients. In surface waters, excess algal production is a major concern.

O

Ocean Discharge Waiver: A variance from Clean Water Act requirements for discharges into marine waters.

Odor Threshold: The minimum odor of a water or air sample that can just be detected after successive dilutions with odorless water. Also called threshold odor.

OECD Guidelines: Testing guidelines prepared by the Organization of Economic and Cooperative Development of the United Nations. They assist in preparation of protocols for studies of toxicology, environmental fate, etc.

Off-Site Facility: A hazardous waste treatment, storage or disposal area that is located away from the generating site.

Office Paper: High grade papers such as copier paper, computer printout, and stationary almost entirely made of uncoated chemical pulp, although some ground wood is used. Such waste is also generated in homes, schools, and elsewhere.

Offsets: A concept whereby emissions from proposed new or modified stationary sources are balanced by reductions from existing sources to stabilize total emissions. (See: bubble, emissions trading, netting)

Offstream Use: Water withdrawn from surface or groundwater sources for use at another place.

Oil and Gas Waste: Gas and oil drilling muds, oil production brines, and other waste associated with exploration for, development and production of crude oil or natural gas.

Oil Desulfurization: Widely used precombustion method for reducing sulfur dioxide emissions from oil-burning power plants. The oil is treated with hydrogen, which removes some of the sulfur by forming hydrogen sulfide gas.

Oil Fingerprinting: A method that identifies sources of oil and allows spills to be traced to their source.

Oil Spill: An accidental or intentional discharge of oil which reaches bodies of water. Can be controlled by chemical dispersion, combustion, mechanical containment, and/or adsorption. Spills from tanks and pipelines can also occur away from water bodies, contaminating the soil, getting into sewer systems and threatening underground water sources.

Oligotrophic Lakes: Deep clear lakes with few nutrients, little organic matter and a high dissolved oxygen level.

On-Scene Coordinator (OSC): The predesignated EPA, Coast Guard, or Department of Defense official who coordinates and directs Superfund removal actions or Clean Water Act oil- or hazardous spill response actions.

On-Site Facility: A hazardous waste treatment, storage or disposal area that is located on the generating site.

Onboard Controls: Devices placed on vehicles to capture gasoline vapor during refueling and route it to the engines when the vehicle is starting so that it can be efficiently burned.

Onconogenicity: The capacity to induce cancer.

One-hit Model: A mathematical model based on the biological theory that a single "hit" of some minimum critical amount of a carcinogen at a cellular target such as DNA can start an irreversible series events leading to a tumor.

Opacity: The amount of light obscured by particulate pollution in the air; clear window glass has zero opacity, a brick wall is 100 percent opaque. Opacity is an indicator of changes in performance of particulate control systems.

Open Burning: Uncontrolled fires in an open dump.

Open Dump: An uncovered site used for disposal of waste without environmental controls.

Operable Unit: Term for each of a number of separate activities undertaken as part of a Superfund site cleanup. A typical operable unit would be removal of drums and tanks from the surface of a site.

Operating Conditions: Conditions specified in a RCRA permit that dictate how an incinerator must operate as it burns different waste types. A trial burn is used to identify operating conditions needed to meet specified performance standards.

Operation and Maintenance: 1. Activities conducted after a Superfund site action is completed to ensure that the action is effective. 2. Actions taken after construction to ensure that facilities constructed to treat waste water will be properly operated and maintained to achieve normative efficiency levels and prescribed effluent limitations in an optimum manner. 3. On-going asbestos management plan in a school or other public building, including regular inspections, various methods of maintaining asbestos in place, and removal when necessary.

Operator Certification: Certification of operators of community and nontransient noncommunity water systems, asbestos specialists, pesticide applicators, hazardous waste transporter, and other such specialists as required by the EPA or a state agency implementing an EPA-approved environmental regulatory program.

Optimal Corrosion Control Treatment: An erosion control treatment that minimizes the lead and copper concentrations at users' taps while also ensuring that the treatment does not cause the water system to violate any national primary drinking water regulations.

Oral Toxicity: Ability of a pesticide to cause injury when ingested.

Organic: 1. Referring to or derived from living organisms. 2. In chemistry, any compound containing carbon.

Organic Chemicals/Compounds: Naturally occuring (animal or plant-produced or synthetic) substances containing mainly carbon, hydrogen, nitrogen, and oxygen.

Organic Matter: Carbonaceous waste contained in plant or animal matter and originating from domestic or industrial sources.

Organism: Any form of animal or plant life.

Organophosphates: Pesticides that contain phosphorus; short-lived, but some can be toxic when first applied.

Organophyllic: A substance that easily combines with organic compounds.

Organotins: Chemical compounds used in anti-foulant paints to protect the hulls of boats and ships, buoys, and pilings from marine organisms such as barnacles.

Original AHERA Inspection/Original Inspection/Inspection: Examination of school buildings arranged by Local Education Agencies to identify asbestos-containing-materials, evaluate their condition, and take samples of materials suspected to contain asbestos; performed by EPA-accredited inspectors.

Original Generation Point: Where regulated medical or other material first becomes waste.

Osmosis: The passage of a liquid from a weak solution to a more concentrated solution across a semipermeable membrane that allows passage of the solvent (water) but not the dissolved solids.

Other Ferrous Metals: Recyclable metals from strapping, furniture, and metal found in tires and consumer electronics but does not include metals found in construction materials or cars, locomotives, and ships. (See: ferrous metals.)

Other Glass: Recyclable glass from furniture, appliances, and consumer electronics. Does not include glass from transportation products (cars trucks or shipping containers) and construction or demolition debris. (See: glass.)

Other Nonferrous Metals: Recyclable nonferrous metals such as lead, copper, and zinc from appliances, consumer electronics, and nonpackaging aluminum products. Does not include nonferrous metals from industrial applications and construction and demolition debris. (See: nonferrous metals.)

Other Paper: For Recyclable paper from books, third-class mail, commercial printing, paper towels, plates and cups; and other nonpackaging paper such as posters, photographic papers, cards and games, milk cartons, folding boxes, bags, wrapping paper, and paperboard. Does not include wrapping paper or shipping cartons.

Other Plastics: Recyclable plastic from appliances, eating utensils, plates, containers, toys, and various kinds of equipment. Does not include heavy-duty plastics such as yielding materials.

Other Solid Waste: Recyclable nonhazardous solid wastes, other than municipal solid waste, covered under Subtitle D of RARA. (See: solid waste.)

Other Wood: Recyclable wood from furniture, consumer electronics cabinets, and other non packaging wood products. Does not include lumber and tree stumps recovered from construction and demolition activities, and industrial process waste such as shavings and sawdust.

Outdoor Air Supply: Air brought into a building from outside.

Outfall: The place where effluent is discharged into receiving waters.

Overburden: Rock and soil cleared away before mining.

Overdraft: The pumping of water from a groundwater basin or aquifer in excess of the supply flowing into the basin; results in a depletion or "mining" of the groundwater in the basin. (See: groundwater mining)

Overfire Air: Air forced into the top of an incinerator or boiler to fan the flames.

Overflow Rate: One of the guidelines for design of the settling tanks and clarifers in a treatment plant; used by plant operators to determine if tanks and clarifiers are over or under-used.

Overland Flow: A land application technique that cleanses waste water by allowing it to flow over a sloped surface. As the water flows over the surface, contaminants are absorbed and the water is collected at the bottom of the slope for reuse.

Oversized Regulated Medical Waste: Medical waste that is too large for plastic bags or standard containers.

Overturn: One complete cycle of top to bottom mixing of previously stratified water masses. This phenomenon may occur in spring or fall, or after storms, and results in uniformity of chemical and physical properties of water at all depths.

Oxidant: A collective term for some of the primary constituents of photochemical smog.

Oxidation Pond: A man-made (anthropogenic) body of water in which waste is consumed by bacteria, used most frequently with other waste-treatment processes; a sewage lagoon.

Oxidation: The chemical addition of oxygen to break down pollutants or organic waste; *e.g.*, destruction of chemicals such as cyanides, phenols, and organic sulfur compounds in sewage by bacterial and chemical means.

Oxidation-Reduction Potential: The electric potential required to transfer electrons from one compound or element (the oxidant) to another compound (the reductant); used as a qualitative measure of the state of oxidation in water treatment systems.

Oxygenated Fuels: Gasoline which has been blended with alcohols or ethers that contain oxygen in order to reduce carbon monoxide and other emissions.

Oxygenated Solvent: An organic solvent containing oxygen as part of the molecular structure. Alcohols and ketones are oxygenated compounds often used as paint solvents.

Ozonation/Ozonator: Application of ozone to water for disinfection or for taste and odor control. The ozonator is the device that does this.

Ozone (O3): Found in two layers of the atmosphere, the stratosphere and the troposphere. In the stratosphere (the atmospheric layer 7 to 10 miles or more above the earth's surface) ozone is a natural form of oxygen that provides a protective layer shielding the earth from ultraviolet radiation. In the troposphere (the layer extending up 7 to 10 miles from the earth's surface), ozone is a chemical oxidant and major component of photochemical smog. It can seriously impair the respiratory system and is one of the most wide- spread of all the criteria pollutants for which the Clean Air Act required EPA to set standards. Ozone in the troposphere is produced through complex chemical reactions of nitrogen oxides, which are among the primary pollutants emitted by combustion sources; hydrocarbons, released into the atmosphere through the combustion, handling and processing of petroleum products; and sunlight.

Ozone Depletion: Destruction of the stratospheric ozone layer which shields the earth from ultraviolet radiation harmful to life. This destruction of ozone is caused by the breakdown of certain chlorine and/or bromine containing compounds (chlorofluorocarbons or halons), which break down when they reach the stratosphere and then catalytically destroy ozone molecules.

Ozone Hole: A thinning break in the stratospheric ozone layer. Designation of amount of such depletion as an "ozone hole" is made when the detected amount of depletion exceeds fifty percent. Seasonal ozone holes have been observed over both the Antarctic and Arctic regions, part of Canada, and the extreme northeastern United States.

Ozone Layer: The protective layer in the atmosphere, about 15 miles above the ground, that absorbs some of the sun's ultraviolet rays, thereby reducing the amount of potentially harmful radiation that reaches the earth's surface.

P

Packaging: The assembly of one or more containers and any other components necessary to ensure minimum compliance with a program's storage and shipment packaging requirements. Also, the containers, etc. involved.

Packed Bed Scrubber: An air pollution control device in which emissions pass through alkaline water to neutralize hydrogen chloride gas.

Packed Tower: A pollution control device that forces dirty air through a tower packed with crushed rock or wood chips while liquid is sprayed over the packing material. The pollutants in the air stream either dissolve or chemically react with the liquid.

Packer: An inflatable gland, or balloon, used to create a temporary seal in a borehole, probe hole, well, or drive casing. It is made of rubber or non-reactive materials.

Palatable Water: Water, at a desirable temperature, that is free from objectionable tastes, odors, colors, and turbidity.

Pandemic: A widespread epidemic throughout an area, nation or the world.

Paper: In the recycling business, refers to products and materials, including newspapers, magazines, office papers, corrugated containers, bags and some paperboard packaging that can be recycled into new paper products.

Paper Processor/Plastics Processor: Intermediate facility where recovered paper or plastic products and materials are sorted, decontaminated, and prepared for final recycling.

Parameter: A variable, measurable property whose value is a determinant of the characteristics of a system; *e.g.* temperature, pressure, and density are parameters of the atmosphere.

Paraquat: A standard herbicide used to kill various types of crops, including marijuana. Causes lung damage if smoke from the crop is inhaled.

Parshall Flume: Device used to measure the flow of water in an open channel.

Part A Permit, Part B Permit: (See: Interim Permit Status.)

Participation Rate: Portion of population participating in a recycling program.

Particle Count: Results of a microscopic examination of treated water with a special "particle counter" that classifies suspended particles by number and size.

Particulate Loading: The mass of particulates per unit volume of air or water.

Particulates: 1. Fine liquid or solid particles such as dust, smoke, mist, fumes, or smog, found in air or emissions. 2. Very small solids suspended in water; they can vary in size, shape, density and electrical charge and can be gathered together by coagulation and flocculation.

Partition Coefficient: Measure of the sorption phenomenon, whereby a pesticide is divided between the soil and water phase; also referred to as adsorption partition coefficient.

Parts Per Billion (ppb)/Parts Per Million (ppm): Units commonly used to express contamination ratios, as in establishing the maximum permissible amount of a contaminant in water, land, or air.

Passive Smoking/Secondhand Smoke: Inhalation of others' tobacco smoke.

Passive Treatment Walls: Technology in which a chemical reaction takes place when contaminated ground water comes in contact with a barrier such as limestone or a wall containing iron filings.

Pathogens: Microorganisms (*e.g.*, bacteria, viruses, or parasites) that can cause disease in humans, animals and plants.

Pathway: The physical course a chemical or pollutant takes from its source to the exposed organism.

Pay-As-You-Throw/Unit-Based Pricing: Systems under which residents pay for municipal waste management and disposal services by weight or volume collected, not a fixed fee.

Peak Electricity Demand: The maximum electricity used to meet the cooling load of a building or buildings in a given area.

Peak Levels: Levels of airborne pollutant contaminants much higher than average or occurring for short periods of time in response to sudden releases.

Percent Saturation: The amount of a substance that is dissolved in a solution compared to the amount that could be dissolved in it.

Perched Water: Zone of unpressurized water held above the water table by impermeable rock or sediment.

Percolating Water: Water that passes through rocks or soil under the force of gravity.

Percolation: 1. The movement of water downward and radially through subsurface soil layers, usually continuing downward to ground water. Can also involve upward movement of water. 2. Slow seepage of water through a filter.

Performance Bond: Cash or securities deposited before a landfill operating permit is issued, which are held to ensure that all requirements for operating ad subsequently closing the landfill are faithful performed. The money is returned to the owner after proper closure of the landfill is completed. If contamination or other problems appear at any time during operation, or upon closure, and are not addressed, the owner must forfeit all or part of the bond which is then used to cover clean-up costs.

Performance Data (For Incinerators): Information collected, during a trial burn, on concentrations of designated organic compounds and pollutants found in incinerator emissions. Data analysis must show that the incinerator meets performance standards under operating conditions specified in the RCRA permit. (See: trial burn; performance standards.)

Performance Standards: 1. Regulatory requirements limiting the concentrations of designated organic compounds, particulate matter, and hydrogen chloride in emissions from incinerators. 2.Operating standards established by EPA for various permitted pollution control systems, asbestos inspections, and various program operations and maintenance requirements.

Periphyton: Microscopic underwater plants and animals that are firmly attached to solid surfaces such as rocks, logs, and pilings.

Permeability: The rate at which liquids pass through soil or other materials in a specified direction.

Permissible Dose: The dose of a chemical that may be received by an individual without the expectation of a significantly harmful result.

Permissible Exposure Limit: Also referred to as PEL, federal limits for workplace exposure to contaminants as established by OSHA.

Permit: An authorization, license, or equivalent control document issued by EPA or an approved state agency to implement the requirements of an environmental regulation; *e.g.* a permit to operate a wastewater treatment plant or to operate a facility that may generate harmful emissions.

Persistence: Refers to the length of time a compound stays in the environment, once introduced. A compound may persist for less than a second or indefinitely.

Persistent Pesticides: Pesticides that do not break down chemically or break down very slowly and remain in the environment after a growing season.

Personal Air Samples: Air samples taken with a pump that is directly attached to the worker with the collecting filter and cassette placed in the worker's breathing zone (required under OSHA asbestos standards and EPA worker protection rule).

Personal Measurement: A measurement collected from an individual's immediate environment.

Personal Protective Equipment: Clothing and equipment worn by pesticide mixers, loaders and applicators and re-entry workers, hazmat emergency responders, workers cleaning up Superfund sites, et. al., which is worn to reduce their exposure to potentially hazardous chemicals and other pollutants.

Pest: An insect, rodent, nematode, fungus, weed or other form of terrestrial or aquatic plant or animal life that is injurious to health or the environment.

Pest Control Operator: Person or company that applies pesticides as a business (*e.g.* exterminator); usually describes household services, not agricultural applications.

Pesticide: Substances or mixture there of intended for preventing, destroying, repelling, or mitigating any pest. Also, any substance or mixture intended for use as a plant regulator, defoliant, or desiccant.

Pesticide Regulation Notice: Formal notice to pesticide registrants about important changes in regulatory policy, procedures, regulations.

Pesticide Tolerance: The amount of pesticide residue allowed by law to remain in or on a harvested crop. EPA sets these levels well below the point where the compounds might be harmful to consumers.

PETE (Polyethylene Terepthalate): Thermoplastic material used in plastic soft drink and rigid containers.

Petroleum: Crude oil or any fraction thereof that is liquid under normal conditions of temperature and pressure. The term includes petroleum-based substances comprising a complex blend of hydrocarbons derived from crude oil through the process of separation, conversion, upgrading, and finishing, such as motor fuel, jet oil, lubricants, petroleum solvents, and used oil.

Petroleum Derivatives: Chemicals formed when gasoline breaks down in contact with ground water.

pH: An expression of the intensity of the basic or acid condition of a liquid; may range from 0 to 14, where 0 is the most acid and 7 is neutral. Natural waters usually have a pH between 6.5 and 8.5.

Pharmacokinetics: The study of the way that drugs move through the body after they are swallowed or injected.

Phenolphthalein Alkalinity: The alkalinity in a water sample measured by the amount of standard acid needed to lower the pH to a level of 8.3 as indicated by the change of color of the phenolphthalein from pink to clear.

Phenols: Organic compounds that are byproducts of petroleum refining, tanning, and textile, dye, and resin manufacturing. Low concentrations cause taste and odor problems in water; higher concentrations can kill aquatic life and humans.

Phosphates: Certain chemical compounds containing phosphorus.

Phosphogypsum Piles (Stacks): Principal byproduct generated in production of phosphoric acid from phosphate rock. These piles may generate radioactive radon gas.

Phosphorus: An essential chemical food element that can contribute to the eutrophication of lakes and other water bodies. Increased phosphorus levels result from discharge of phosphorus-containing materials into surface waters.

Phosphorus Plants: Facilities using electric furnaces to produce elemental phosphorous for commercial use, such as high grade phosphoric acid, phosphate-based detergent, and organic chemicals use.

Photochemical Oxidants: Air pollutants formed by the action of sunlight on oxides of nitrogen and hydrocarbons.

Photochemical Smog: Air pollution caused by chemical reactions of various pollutants emitted from different sources. (See: photochemical oxidants.)

Photosynthesis: The manufacture by plants of carbohydrates and oxygen from carbon dioxide mediated by chlorophyll in the presence of sunlight.

Physical and Chemical Treatment: Processes generally used in large-scale wastewater treatment facilities. Physical processes may include air-stripping or filtration. Chemical treatment includes coagulation, chlorination, or ozonation. The term can also refer to treatment of toxic materials in surface and ground waters, oil spills, and some methods of dealing with hazardous materials on or in the ground.

Phytoplankton: That portion of the plankton community comprised of tiny plants; *e.g.* algae, diatoms.

Phytoremediation: Low-cost remediation option for sites with widely dispersed contamination at low concentrations.

Phytotoxic: Harmful to plants.

Phytotreatment: The cultivation of specialized plants that absorb specific contaminants from the soil through their roots or foliage. This reduces the concentration of contaminants in the soil, but incorporates them into biomasses that may be released back into the environment when the plant dies or is harvested.

Picocuries Per Liter pCi/L): A unit of measure for levels of radon gas; becquerels per cubic meter is metric equivalent.

Piezometer: A nonpumping well, generally of small diameter, for measuring the elevation of a water table.

Pilot Tests: Testing a cleanup technology under actual site conditions to identify potential problems prior to full-scale implementation.

Plankton: Tiny plants and animals that live in water.

Plasma Arc Reactors: devices that use an electric arc to thermally decompose organic and inorganic materials at ultra-high temperatures into gases and a vitrified slag residue. A plasma arc reactor can operate as any of the following:

- integral component of chemical, fuel, or electricity production systems, processing high or medium value organic compounds into a synthetic gas used as a fuel
- materials recovery device, processing scrap to recover metal from the slag
- destruction or incineration system, processing waste materials into slag and gases ignited inside of a secondary combustion chamber that follows the reactor

Plasmid: A circular piece of DNA that exists apart from the chromosome and replicates independently of it. Bacterial plasmids carry information that renders the bacteria resistant to antibiotics. Plasmids are often used in genetic engineering to carry desired genes into organisms.

Plastics: Non-metallic chemoreactive compounds molded into rigid or pliable construction materials, fabrics, etc.

Plate Tower Scrubber: An air pollution control device that neutralizes hydrogen chloride gas by bubbling alkaline water through holes in a series of metal plates.

Plug Flow: Type of flow the occurs in tanks, basins, or reactors when a slug of water moves through without ever dispersing or mixing with the rest of the water flowing through.

Plugging: Act or process of stopping the flow of water, oil, or gas into or out of a formation through a borehole or well penetrating that formation.

Plume: 1. A visible or measurable discharge of a contaminant from a given point of origin. Can be visible or thermal in water, or visible in the air as, for example, a plume of smoke; 2. The area of radiation leaking from a damaged reactor; 3. Area downwind within which a release could be dangerous for those exposed to leaking fumes.

Plutonium: A radioactive metallic element chemically similar to uranium.

PM-10/PM-2.5: PM 10 is measure of particles in the atmosphere with a diameter of less than ten or equal to a nominal 10 micrometers. PM-2.5 is a measure of smaller particles in the air. PM-10 has been the pollutant particulate level standard against which EPA has been measuring Clean Air Act compliance. On the basis of newer scientific findings, the Agency is considering regulations that will make PM-2.5 the new "standard".

Pneumoconiosis: Health conditions characterized by permanent deposition of substantial amounts of particulate matter in the lungs and by the tissue reaction to its presence; can range from relatively harmless forms of sclerosis to the destructive fibrotic effect of silicosis.

Point Source: A stationary location or fixed facility from which pollutants are discharged; any single identifiable source of pollution; *e.g.* a pipe, ditch, ship, ore pit, factory smokestack.

Point-of-Contact Measurement of Exposure: Estimating exposure by measuring concentrations over time (while the exposure is taking place) at or near the place where it is occurring.

Point-of-Disinfectant Application: The point where disinfectant is applied and water downstream of that point is not subject to recontamination by surface water runoff.

Point-of-Use Treatment Device: Treatment device applied to a single tap to reduce contaminants in the drinking water at the one faucet.

Pollen: The fertilizing element of flowering plants; background air pollutant.

Pollutant: Generally, any substance introduced into the environment that adversely affects the usefulness of a resource or the health of humans, animals, or ecosystems.

Pollutant Pathways: Avenues for distribution of pollutants. In most buildings, for example, HVAC systems are the primary pathways although all building components can interact to affect how air movement distributes pollutants.

Pollutant Standard Index (PSI): Indicator of one or more pollutants that may be used to inform the public about the potential for adverse health effects from air pollution in major cities.

Pollution: Generally, the presence of a substance in the environment that because of its chemical composition or quantity prevents the functioning of natural processes and produces undesirable environmental and health effects. Under the Clean Water Act, for example, the term has been defined as the man-made or man-induced alteration of the physical, biological, chemical, and radiological integrity of water and other media.

Pollution Prevention: 1. Identifying areas, processes, and activities which create excessive waste products or pollutants in order to reduce or prevent them through, alteration, or eliminating a process. Such activities, consistent with the Pollution Prevention Act of 1990, are conducted across all EPA programs and can involve cooperative efforts with such agencies as the Departments of Agriculture and Energy.

2. EPA has initiated a number of voluntary programs in which industrial, or commercial or "partners" join with EPA in promoting activities that conserve energy, conserve and protect water supply, reduce emissions or find ways of utilizing them as energy resources, and reduce the waste stream. Among these are: Agstar, to reduce methane emissions through manure management. Climate Wise, to lower industrial greenhouse-gas emissions and energy costs. Coalbed Methane Outreach, to boost methane recovery at coal mines. Design for the Environment, to foster including environmental considerations in product design and processes. Energy Star programs, to promote energy efficiency in commercial and residential buildings, office equipment, transformers, computers, office equipment, and home appliances. Environmental Accounting, to help businesses identify environmental costs and factor them into management decision making. Green Chemistry, to promote and recognize cost-effective breakthroughs in chemistry that prevent pollution. Green Lights, to spread the use of energy-efficient lighting technologies. Indoor Environments, to reduce risks from indoor-air pollution. Landfill Methane Outreach, to develop landfill gas-to-energy projects. Natural Gas Star, to reduce methane emissions from the natural gas industry. Ruminant Livestock Methane, to reduce methane emissions from ruminant livestock. Transportation Partners, to reduce carbon dioxide emissions from the transportation sector. Voluntary Aluminum Industrial Partnership, to reduce per fluorocarbon emissions from the primary aluminum industry. WAVE, to promote efficient water use in the lodging industry. Wastewise, to reduce business-generated solid waste through prevention, reuse, and recycling. (See: Common Sense Initiative and Project XL.)

Polychlorinated Biphenyls: A group of toxic, persistent chemicals used in electrical transformers and capacitors for insulating purposes, and in gas pipeline systems as lubricant. The sale and new use of these chemicals, also known as PCBs, were banned by law in 1979.

Portal-of-Entry Effect: A local effect produced in the tissue or organ of first contact between a toxicant and the biological system.

Polonium: A radioactive element that occurs in pitchblende and other uranium-containing ores.

Polyelectrolytes: Synthetic chemicals that help solids to clump during sewage treatment.

Polymer: A natural or synthetic chemical structure where two or more like molecules are joined to form a more complex molecular structure (*e.g.* polyethylene in plastic).

Polyvinyl Chloride (PVC): A tough, environmentally indestructible plastic that releases hydrochloric acid when burned.

Population: A group of interbreeding organisms occupying a particular space; the number of humans or other living creatures in a designated area.

Population at Risk: A population subgroup that is more likely to be exposed to a chemical, or is more sensitive to the chemical, than is the general population.

Porosity: Degree to which soil, gravel, sediment, or rock is permeated with pores or cavities through which water or air can move.

Post-Chlorination: Addition of chlorine to plant effluent for disinfectant purposes after the effluent has been treated.

Post-Closure: The time period following the shutdown of a waste management or manufacturing facility; for monitoring purposes, often considered to be 30 years.

Post-Consumer Materials/Waste: Materials or finished products that have served their intended use and have been diverted or recovered from waste destined for disposal, having completed their lives as consumer items. Postconsumer materials are part of the broader category of recovered materials.

Post-Consumer Recycling: Use of materials generated from residential and consumer waste for new or similar purposes; *e.g.*

converting wastepaper from offices into corrugated boxes or newsprint.

Potable Water: Water that is safe for drinking and cooking.

Potential Dose: The amount of a compound contained in material swallowed, breathed, or applied to the skin.

Potentially Responsible Party (PRP): Any individual or company—including owners, operators, transporters or generators—potentially responsible for, or contributing to a spill or other contamination at a Superfund site. Whenever possible, through administrative and legal actions, EPA requires PRPs to clean up hazardous sites they have contaminated.

Potentiation: The ability of one chemical to increase the effect of another chemical.

Potentiometric Surface: The surface to which water in an aquifer can rise by hydrostatic pressure.

Precautionary Principle: When information about potential risks is incomplete, basing decisions about the best ways to manage or reduce risks on a preference for avoiding unnecessary health risks instead of on unnecessary economic expenditures.

Pre-Consumer Materials/Waste: Materials generated in manufacturing and converting processes such as manufacturing scrap and trimmings and cuttings. Includes print overruns, overissue publications, and obsolete inventories.

Pre-Harvest Interval: The time between the last pesticide application and harvest of the treated crops.

Prechlorination: The addition of chlorine at the headworks of a treatment plant prior to other treatment processes. Done mainly for disinfection and control of tastes, odors, and aquatic growths, and to aid in coagulation and settling.

Precipitate: A substance separated from a solution or suspension by chemical or physical change.

Precipitation: Removal of hazardous solids from liquid waste to permit safe disposal; removal of particles from airborne emissions as in rain (*e.g.* acid precipitation).

Precipitator: Pollution control device that collects particles from an air stream.

Precursor: In photochemistry, a compound antecedent to a pollutant. For example, volatile organic compounds (VOCs) and nitric oxides of nitrogen react in sunlight to form ozone or other photochemical oxidants. As such, VOCs and oxides of nitrogen are precursors.

Preliminary Assessment: The process of collecting and reviewing available information about a known or suspected waste site or release.

Prescriptive: Water rights which are acquired by diverting water and putting it to use in accordance with specified procedures; *e.g.* filing a request with a state agency to use unused water in a stream, river, or lake.

Pressed Wood Products: Materials used in building and furniture construction that are made from wood veneers, particles, or fibers bonded together with an adhesive under heat and pressure.

Pressure Sewers: A system of pipes in which water, wastewater, or other liquid is pumped to a higher elevation.

Pressure, Static: In flowing air, the total pressure minus velocity pressure, pushing equally in all directions.

Pressure, Total: In flowing air, the sum of the static and velocity pressures.

Pressure, Velocity: In flowing air, the pressure due to velocity and density of air.

Pretreatment: Processes used to reduce, eliminate, or alter the nature of wastewater pollutants from non-domestic sources before they are discharged into publicly owned treatment works (POTWs).

Prevalent Level Samples: Air samples taken under normal conditions (also known as ambient background samples).

Prevalent Levels: Levels of airborne contaminant occurring under normal conditions.

Prevention of Significant Deterioration (PSD): EPA program in which state and/or federal permits are required in order to restrict emissions from new or modified sources in places where air quality already meets or exceeds primary and secondary ambient air quality standards.

Primacy: Having the primary responsibility for administering and enforcing regulations.

Primary Drinking Water Regulation: Applies to public water systems and specifies a contaminant level, which, in the judgment of the EPA Administrator, will not adversely affect human health.

Primary Effect: An effect where the stressor acts directly on the ecological component of interest, not on other parts of the ecosystem. (See: secondary effect.)

Primary Standards: National ambient air quality standards designed to protect human health with an adequate margin for safety. (See: National Ambient Air Quality Standards, secondary standards.)

Primary Treatment: First stage of wastewater treatment in which solids are removed by screening and settling.

Primary Waste Treatment: First steps in wastewater treatment; screens and sedimentation tanks are used to remove most materials that float or will settle. Primary treatment removes about 30 percent of carbonaceous biochemical oxygen demand from domestic sewage.

Principal Organic Hazardous Constituents (POHCs): Hazardous compounds monitored during an incinerator's trial burn, selected for high concentration in the waste feed and difficulty of combustion.

Prions: Microscopic particles made of protein that can cause disease.

Prior Appropriation: A doctrine of water law that allocates the rights to use water on a first-come, first-served basis.

Probability of Detection: The likelihood, expressed as a percentage, that a test method will correctly identify a leaking tank.

Process Variable: A physical or chemical quantity which is usually measured and controlled in the operation of a water treatment plant or industrial plant.

Process Verification: Verifying that process raw materials, water usage, waste treatment processes, production rate and other facts relative to quantity and quality of pollutants contained in discharges are substantially described in the permit application and the issued permit.

Process Wastewater: Any water that comes into contact with any raw material, product, byproduct, or waste.

Process Weight: Total weight of all materials, including fuel, used in a manufacturing process; used to calculate the allowable particulate emission rate.

Producers: Plants that perform photosynthesis and provide food to consumers.

Product Level: The level of a product in a storage tank.

Product Water: Water that has passed through a water treatment plant and is ready to be delivered to consumers.

Products of Incomplete Combustion (PICs): Organic compounds formed by combustion. Usually generated in small amounts and sometimes toxic, PICs are heat-altered versions of the original material fed into the incinerator (*e.g.* charcoal is a P.I.C. from burning wood).

Project XL: An EPA initiative to give states and the regulated community the flexibility to develop comprehensive strategies as alternatives to multiple current regulatory requirements in order to exceed compliance and increase overall environmental benefits.

Propellant: Liquid in a self-pressurized pesticide product that expels the active ingredient from its container.

Proportionate Mortality Ratio (PMR): The number of deaths from a specific cause in a specific period of time per 100 deaths from all causes in the same time period.

Proposed Plan: A plan for a site cleanup that is available to the public for comment.

Proteins: Complex nitrogenous organic compounds of high molecular weight made of amino acids; essential for growth and repair of animal tissue. Many, but not all, proteins are enzymes.

Protocol: A series of formal steps for conducting a test.

Protoplast: A membrane-bound cell from which the outer wall has been partially or completely removed. The term often is applied to plant cells.

Protozoa: One-celled animals that are larger and more complex than bacteria. May cause disease.

Public Comment Period: The time allowed for the public to express its views and concerns regarding an action by EPA (*e.g.* a Federal Register Notice of proposed rule-making, a public notice of a draft permit, or a Notice of Intent to Deny).

Public Health Approach: Regulatory and voluntary focus on effective and feasible risk management actions at the national and community level to reduce human exposures and risks, with priority given to reducing exposures with the biggest impacts in terms of the number affected and severity of effect.

Public Health Context: The incidence, prevalence, and severity of diseases in communities or populations and the factors that account for them, including infections, exposure to pollutants, and other exposures or activities.

Public Hearing: A formal meeting wherein EPA officials hear the public's views and concerns about an EPA action or proposal. EPA is required to consider such comments when evaluating its actions. Public hearings must be held upon request during the public comment period.

Public Notice: 1. Notification by EPA informing the public of Agency actions such as the issuance of a draft permit or scheduling of a hearing. EPA is required to ensure proper public notice, including publication in newspapers and broadcast over radio and television stations. 2. In the safe drinking water program, water suppliers are required to publish and broadcast notices when pollution problems are discovered.

Public Water System: A system that provides piped water for human consumption to at least 15 service connections or regularly serves 25 individuals.

Publicly Owned Treatment Works (POTWs): A waste-treatment works owned by a state, unit of local government, or Indian tribe, usually designed to treat domestic wastewaters.

Pumping Station: Mechanical device installed in sewer or water system or other liquid-carrying pipelines to move the liquids to a higher level.

Pumping Test: A test conducted to determine aquifer or well characteristics.

Purging: Removing stagnant air or water from sampling zone or equipment prior to sample collection.

Putrefaction: Biological decomposition of organic matter; associated with anaerobic conditions.

Putrescible: Able to rot quickly enough to cause odors and attract flies.

Pyrolysis: Decomposition of a chemical by extreme heat.

Q

Qualitative Use Assessment: Report summarizing the major uses of a pesticide including percentage of crop treated, and amount of pesticide used on a site.

Quality Assurance/Quality Control: A system of procedures, checks, audits, and corrective actions to ensure that all EPA research design and performance, environmental monitoring and sampling, and other technical and reporting activities are of the highest achievable quality.

Quench Tank: A water-filled tank used to cool incinerator residues or hot materials during industrial processes.

R

Radiation: Transmission of energy though space or any medium. Also known as radiant energy.

Radiation Standards: Regulations that set maximum exposure limits for protection of the public from radioactive materials.

Radio Frequency Radiation: (See non-ionizing electromagnetic radiation.)

Radioactive Decay: Spontaneous change in an atom by emission of of charged particles and/or gamma rays; also known as radioactive disintegration and radioactivity.

Radioactive Substances: Substances that emit ionizing radiation.

Radioactive Waste: Any waste that emits energy as rays, waves, streams or energetic particles. Radioactive materials are often mixed with hazardous waste, from nuclear reactors, research institutions, or hospitals.

Radioisotopes: Chemical variants of radioactive elements with potentially oncogenic, teratogenic, and mutagenic effects on the human body.

Radionuclide: Radioactive particle, man-made (anthropogenic) or natural, with a distinct atomic weight number. Can have a long life as soil or water pollutant.

Radius of Vulnerability Zone: The maximum distance from the point of release of a hazardous substance in which the airborne concentration could reach the level of concern under specified weather conditions.

Radius of Influence: 1. The radial distance from the center of a wellbore to the point where there is no lowering of the water table or potentiometric surface (the edge of the cone of depression); 2. the radial distance from an extraction well that has adequate air flow for effective removal of contaminants when a vacuum is applied to the extraction well.

Radon: A colorless naturally occurring, radioactive, inert gas formed by radioactive decay of radium atoms in soil or rocks.

Radon Daughters/Radon Progeny: Short-lived radioactive decay products of radon that decay into longer-lived lead isotopes that can attach themselves to airborne dust and other particles and, if inhaled, damage the linings of the lungs.

Radon Decay Products: A term used to refer collectively to the immediate products of the radon decay chain. These include Po-218, Pb-214, Bi-214, and Po-214, which have an average combined half-life of about 30 minutes.

Rainbow Report: Comprehensive document giving the status of all pesticides now or ever in registration or special reviews. Known as the "rainbow report" because chapters are printed on different colors of paper.

Rasp: A machine that grinds waste into a manageable material and helps prevent odor.

Raw Agricultural Commodity: An unprocessed human food or animal feed crop (*e.g.*, raw carrots, apples, corn, or eggs.)

Raw Sewage: Untreated wastewater and its contents.

Raw Water: Intake water prior to any treatment or use.

Re-entry: (In indoor air program) Refers to air exhausted from a building that is immediately brought back into the system through the air intake and other openings.

Reactivity: Refers to those hazardous wastes that are normally unstable and readily undergo violent chemical change but do not explode.

Reaeration: Introduction of air into the lower layers of a reservoir. As the air bubbles form and rise through the water, the oxygen dissolves into the water and replenishes the dissolved oxygen. The rising bubbles also cause the lower waters to rise to the surface where they take on oxygen from the atmosphere.

Real-Time Monitoring: Monitoring and measuring environmental developments with technology and communications systems that provide time-relevant information to the public in an easily understood format people can use in day-to-day decision-making about their health and the environment.

Reasonable Further Progress: Annual incremental reductions in air pollutant emissions as reflected in a State Implementation Plan that EPA deems sufficient to provide for the attainment of the applicable national ambient air quality standards by the statutory deadline.

Reasonable Maximum Exposure: The maximum exposure reasonably expected to occur in a population.

Reasonable Worst Case: An estimate of the individual dose, exposure, or risk level received by an individual in a defined population that is greater than the 90th percentile but less than that received by anyone in the 98th percentile in the same population.

Reasonably Available Control Measures (RACM): A broadly defined term referring to technological and other measures for pollution control.

Reasonably Available Control Technology (RACT): Control technology that is reasonably available, and both technologically and economically feasible. Usually applied to existing sources in nonattainment areas; in most cases is less stringent than new source performance standards.

Recarbonization: Process in which carbon dioxide is bubbled into water being treated to lower the pH.

Receiving Waters: A river, lake, ocean, stream or other watercourse into which wastewater or treated effluent is discharged.

Receptor: Ecological entity exposed to a stressor.

Recharge: The process by which water is added to a zone of saturation, usually by percolation from the soil surface; *e.g.*, the recharge of an aquifer.

Recharge Area: A land area in which water reaches the zone of saturation from surface infiltration, *e.g.*, where rainwater soaks through the earth to reach an aquifer.

Recharge Rate: The quantity of water per unit of time that replenishes or refills an aquifer.

Reclamation: (In recycling) Restoration of materials found in the waste stream to a beneficial use which may be for purposes other than the original use.

Recombinant Bacteria: A microorganism whose genetic makeup has been altered by deliberate introduction of new genetic elements. The offspring of these altered bacteria also contain these new genetic elements; *i.e.* they "breed true."

Recombinant DNA: The new DNA that is formed by combining pieces of DNA from different organisms or cells.

Recommended Maximum Contaminant Level (RMCL): The maximum level of a contaminant in drinking water at which no known or anticipated adverse effect on human health would occur, and that includes an adequate margin of safety. Recommended levels are nonenforceable health goals. (See: maximum contaminant level.)

Reconstructed Source: Facility in which components are replaced to such an extent that the fixed capital cost of the new components exceeds 50 percent of the capital cost of constructing a comparable brand-new facility. New-source performance standards may be applied to sources reconstructed after the proposal of the standard if it is technologically and economically feasible to meet the standards.

Reconstruction of Dose: Estimating exposure after it has occurred by using evidence within an organism such as chemical levels in tissue or fluids.

Record of Decision (ROD): A public document that explains which cleanup alternative(s) will be used at National Priorities List sites where, under CERCLA, Trust Funds pay for the cleanup.

Recovery Rate: Percentage of usable recycled materials that have been removed from the total amount of municipal solid waste generated in a specific area or by a specific business.

Recycle/Reuse: Minimizing waste generation by recovering and reprocessing usable products that might otherwise become waste (*.i.e.* recycling of aluminum cans, paper, and bottles, etc.).

Recycling and Reuse Business Assistance Centers: Located in state solid-waste or economic development agencies, these centers provide recycling businesses with customized and targeted assistance.

Recycling Economic Development Advocates: Individuals hired by state or tribal economic development offices to focus financial, marketing, and permitting resources on creating recycling businesses.

Recycling Mill: Facility where recovered materials are remanufactured into new products.

Recycling Technical Assistance Partnership National Network: A national information-sharing resource designed to help businesses and manufacturers increase their use of recovered materials.

Red Bag Waste: (See: infectious waste.)

Red Border: An EPA document undergoing review before being submitted for final management decision-making.

Red Tide: A proliferation of a marine plankton toxic and often fatal to fish, perhaps stimulated by the addition of nutrients. A tide can be red, green, or brown, depending on the coloration of the plankton.

Redemption Program: Program in which consumers are monetarily compensated for the collection of recyclable materials, generally through prepaid deposits or taxes on beverage containers. In some states or localities legislation has enacted redemption programs to help prevent roadside litter. (See:bottle bill.)

Reduction: The addition of hydrogen, removal of oxygen, or addition of electrons to an element or compound.

Reentry Interval: The period of time immediately following the application of a pesticide during which unprotected workers should not enter a field.

Reference Dose (RfD): The RfD is a numerical estimate of a daily oral exposure to the human population, including sensitive subgroups such as children, that is not likely to cause harmful effects during a lifetime. RfDs are generally used for health effects that are thought to have a threshold or low dose limit for producing effects.

Reformulated Gasoline: Gasoline with a different composition from conventional gasoline (*e.g.*, lower aromatics content) that cuts air pollutants.

Refueling Emissions: Emissions released during vehicle re-fueling.

Refuse Reclamation: Conversion of solid waste into useful products; *e.g.*, composting organic wastes to make soil conditioners or separating aluminum and other metals for recycling.

Regeneration: Manipulation of cells to cause them to develop into whole plants.

Regional Response Team (RRT): Representatives of federal, local, and state agencies who may assist in coordination of activities at the request of the On-Scene Coordinator before and during a significant pollution incident such as an oil spill, major chemical release, or Superfund response.

Registrant: Any manufacturer or formulator who obtains registration for a pesticide active ingredient or product.

Registration: Formal listing with EPA of a new pesticide before it can be sold or distributed. Under the Federal Insecticide, Fungicide, and Rodenticide Act, EPA is responsible for registration (pre-market licensing) of pesticides on the basis of data demonstrating no unreasonable adverse effects on human health or the environment when applied according to approved label directions.

Registration Standards: Published documents which include summary reviews of the data available on a pesticide's active ingredient, data gaps, and the Agency's existing regulatory position on the pesticide.

Regulated Asbestos-Containing Material (RACM): Friable asbestos material or nonfriable ACM that will be or has been subjected to sanding, grinding, cutting, or abrading or has crumbled, or been pulverized or reduced to powder in the course of demolition or renovation operations.

Regulated Medical Waste: Under the Medical Waste Tracking Act of 1988, any solid waste generated in the diagnosis, treatment, or immunization of human beings or animals, in research pertaining thereto, or in the production or testing of biologicals. Included are cultures and stocks of infectious agents; human blood and blood products; human pathological body wastes from surgery and autopsy; contaminated animal carcasses from medical research; waste from patients with communicable diseases; and all used sharp implements, such as needles and scalpels, and certain unused sharps. (See: treated medical waste; untreated medical waste; destroyed medical waste.)

Relative Ecological Sustainability: Ability of an ecosystem to maintain relative ecological integrity indefinitely.

Relative Permeability: The permeability of a rock to gas, NAIL, or water, when any two or more are present.

Relative Risk Assessment: Estimating the risks associated with different stressors or management actions.

Release: Any spilling, leaking, pumping, pouring, emitting, emptying, discharging, injecting, escaping, leaching, dumping, or disposing into the environment of a hazardous or toxic chemical or extremely hazardous substance.

Remedial Action (RA): The actual construction or implementation phase of a Superfund site cleanup that follows remedial design.

Remedial Design: A phase of remedial action that follows the remedial investigation/feasibility study and includes development of engineering drawings and specifications for a site cleanup.

Remedial Investigation: An in-depth study designed to gather data needed to determine the nature and extent of contamination at a Superfund site; establish site cleanup criteria; identify preliminary alternatives for remedial action; and support technical and cost analyses of alternatives. The remedial investigation is usually done with the feasibility study. Together they are usually referred to as the "RI/FS".

Remedial Project Manager (RPM): The EPA or state official responsible for overseeing on-site remedial action.

Remedial Response: Long-term action that stops or substantially reduces a release or threat of a release of hazardous substances that is serious but not an immediate threat to public health.

Remediation: 1. Cleanup or other methods used to remove or contain a toxic spill or hazardous materials from a Superfund site; 2. for the Asbestos Hazard Emergency Response program, abatement methods including evaluation, repair, enclosure, encapsulation, or removal of greater than 3 linear feet or square feet of asbestos-containing materials from a building.

Remote Sensing: The collection and interpretation of information about an object without physical contact with the object; *e.g.*, satellite imaging, aerial photography, and open path measurements.

Removal Action: Short-term immediate actions taken to address releases of hazardous substances that require expedited response. (See: cleanup.)

Renewable Energy Production Incentive (REPI): Incentive established by the Energy Policy Act available to renewable energy power projects owned by a state or local government or nonprofit electric cooperative.

Repeat Compliance Period: Any subsequent compliance period after the initial one.

Reportable Quantity (RQ): Quantity of a hazardous substance that triggers reports under CERCLA. If a substance exceeds its RQ, the release must be reported to the National Response Center, the SERC, and community emergency coordinators for areas likely to be affected.

Repowering: Rebuilding and replacing major components of a power plant instead of building a new one.

Representative Sample: A portion of material or water that is as nearly identical in content and consistency as possible to that in the larger body of material or water being sampled.

Reregistration: The reevaluation and relicensing of existing pesticides originally registered prior to current scientific and regulatory standards. EPA reregisters pesticides through its Registration Standards Program.

Reserve Capacity: Extra treatment capacity built into solid waste and wastewater treatment plants and interceptor sewers to accommodate flow increases due to future population growth.

Reservoir: Any natural or artificial holding area used to store, regulate, or control water.

Residential Use: Pesticide application in and around houses, office buildings, apartment buildings, motels, and other living or working areas.

Residential Waste: Waste generated in single and multi-family homes, including newspapers, clothing, disposable tableware, food packaging, cans, bottles, food scraps, and yard trimmings other than those that are diverted to backyard composting. (See: Household hazardous waste.)

Residual: Amount of a pollutant remaining in the environment after a natural or technological process has taken place; *e.g.*, the sludge remaining after initial wastewater treatment, or particulates remaining in air after it passes through a scrubbing or other process.

Residual Risk: The extent of health risk from air pollutants remaining after application of the Maximum Achievable Control Technology (MACT).

Residual Saturation: Saturation level below which fluid drainage will not occur.

Residue: The dry solids remaining after the evaporation of a sample of water or sludge.

Resistance: For plants and animals, the ability to withstand poor environmental conditions or attacks by chemicals or disease. May be inborn or acquired.

Resource Recovery: The process of obtaining matter or energy from materials formerly discarded.

Response Action: 1. Generic term for actions taken in response to actual or potential health threatening environmental events such as spills, sudden releases, and asbestos abatement/management problems. 2. A CERCLA-authorized action involving either a short-term removal action or a long-term removal response. This may include but is not limited to: removing hazardous materials from a site to an EPA-approved hazardous waste facility for treatment, containment or treating the waste on-site, identifying and removing the sources of ground-water contamination and halting further migration of contaminants. 3. Any of the following actions taken in school buildings in response to AHERA to reduce the risk of exposure to asbestos: removal, encapsulation, enclosure, repair, and operations and maintenance. (See: cleanup.)

Responsiveness Summary: A summary of oral and/or written public comments received by EPA during a comment period on key EPA documents, and EPA's response to those comments.

Restoration: Measures taken to return a site to pre-violation conditions.

Restricted Entry Interval: The time after a pesticide application during which entry into the treated area is restricted.

Restricted Use: A pesticide may be classified (under FIFRA regulations) for restricted use if it requires special handling because of its toxicity, and, if so, it may be applied only by trained, certified applicators or those under their direct supervision.

Restriction Enzymes: Enzymes that recognize specific regions of a long DNA molecule and cut it at those points.

Retrofit: Addition of a pollution control device on an existing facility without making major changes to the generating plant. Also called backfit.

Reuse: Using a product or component of municipal solid waste in its original form more than once; *e.g.*, refilling a glass bottle that has been returned or using a coffee can to hold nuts and bolts.

Reverse Osmosis: A treatment process used in water systems by adding pressure to force water through a semi-permeable membrane. Reverse osmosis removes most drinking water contaminants. Also used in wastewater treatment. Large-scale reverse osmosis plants are being developed.

Reversible Effect: An effect which is not permanent; especially adverse effects which diminish when exposure to a toxic chemical stops.

Ribonucleic Acid (RNA): A molecule that carries the genetic message from DNA to a cellular protein-producing mechanism.

Rill: A small channel eroded into the soil by surface runoff; can be easily smoothed out or obliterated by normal tillage.

Ringlemann Chart: A series of shaded illustrations used to measure the opacity of air pollution emissions, ranging from light grey through black; used to set and enforce emissions standards.

Riparian Habitat: Areas adjacent to rivers and streams with a differing density, diversity, and productivity of plant and animal species relative to nearby uplands.

Riparian Rights: Entitlement of a land owner to certain uses of water on or bordering the property, including the right to prevent diversion or misuse of upstream waters. Generally a matter of state law.

Risk: A measure of the probability that damage to life, health, property, and/or the environment will occur as a result of a given hazard.

Risk (Adverse) for Endangered Species: Risk to aquatic species if anticipated pesticide residue levels equal one-fifth of LD10 or one-tenth of LC50; risk to terrestrial species if anticipated pesticide residue levels equal one-fifth of LC10 or one-tenth of LC50.

Risk Assessment: Qualitative and quantitative evaluation of the risk posed to human health and/or the environment by the actual or potential presence and/or use of specific pollutants.

Risk Characterization: The last phase of the risk assessment process that estimates the potential for adverse health or ecological effects to occur from exposure to a stressor and evaluates the uncertainty involved.

Risk Communication: The exchange of information about health or environmental risks among risk assessors and managers, the general public, news media, interest groups, etc.

Risk Estimate: A description of the probability that organisms exposed to a specific dose of a chemical or other pollutant will develop an adverse response, *e.g.*, cancer.

Risk Factor: Characteristics (*e.g.*, race, sex, age, obesity) or variables (*e.g.*, smoking, occupational exposure level) associated with increased probability of a toxic effect.

Risk for Non-Endangered Species: Risk to species if anticipated pesticide residue levels are equal to or greater than LC50.

Risk Management: The process of evaluating and selecting alternative regulatory and non-regulatory responses to risk. The selection process necessarily requires the consideration of legal, economic, and behavioral factors.

Risk-based Targeting: The direction of resources to those areas that have been identified as having the highest potential or actual adverse effect on human health and/or the environment.

Risk-Specific Dose: The dose associated with a specified risk level.

River Basin: The land area drained by a river and its tributaries.

Rodenticide: A chemical or agent used to destroy rats or other rodent pests, or to prevent them from damaging food, crops, etc.

Rotary Kiln Incinerator: An incinerator with a rotating combustion chamber that keeps waste moving, thereby allowing it to vaporize for easier burning.

Rough Fish: Fish not prized for sport or eating, such as gar and suckers. Most are more tolerant of changing environmental conditions than are game or food species.

Route of Exposure: The avenue by which a chemical comes into contact with an organism, *e.g.*, inhalation, ingestion, dermal contact, injection.

Rubbish: Solid waste, excluding food waste and ashes, from homes, institutions, and workplaces.

Run-Off: That part of precipitation, snow melt, or irrigation water that runs off the land into streams or other surface-water. It can carry pollutants from the air and land into receiving waters.

Running Losses: Evaporation of motor vehicle fuel from the fuel tank while the vehicle is in use.

S

Sacrifical Anode: An easily corroded material deliberately installed in a pipe or intake to give it up (sacrifice it) to corrosion while the rest of the water supply facility remains relatively corrosion-free.

Safe: Condition of exposure under which there is a practical certainty that no harm will result to exposed individuals.

Safe Water: Water that does not contain harmful bacteria, toxic materials, or chemicals, and is considered safe for drinking even if it may have taste, odor, color, and certain mineral problems.

Safe Yield: The annual amount of water that can be taken from a source of supply over a period of years without depleting that source beyond its ability to be replenished naturally in "wet years."

Safener: A chemical added to a pesticide to keep it from injuring plants.

Salinity: The percentage of salt in water.

Salt Water Intrusion: The invasion of fresh surface or ground water by salt water. If it comes from the ocean it may be called sea water intrusion.

Salts: Minerals that water picks up as it passes through the air, over and under the ground, or from households and industry.

Salvage: The utilization of waste materials.

Sampling Frequency: The interval between the collection of successive samples.

Sanctions: Actions taken by the federal government for failure to provide or implement a State Implementation Plan (SIP). Such action may include withholding of highway funds and a ban on construction of new sources of potential pollution.

Sand Filters: Devices that remove some suspended solids from sewage. Air and bacteria decompose additional wastes filtering through the sand so that cleaner water drains from the bed.

Sanitary Sewers: Underground pipes that carry off only domestic or industrial waste, not storm water.

Sanitary Survey: An on-site review of the water sources, facilities, equipment, operation and maintenance of a public water system to evaluate the adequacy of those elements for producing and distributing safe drinking water.

Sanitary Water (Also known as gray water): Water discharged from sinks, showers, kitchens, or other non-industrial operations, but not from commodes.

Sanitation: Control of physical factors in the human environment that could harm development, health, or survival.

Saprolite: A soft, clay-rich, thoroughly decomposed rock formed in place by chemical weathering of igneous or metamorphic rock. Forms in humid, tropical, or subtropical climates.

Saprophytes: Organisms living on dead or decaying organic matter that help natural decomposition of organic matter in water.

Saturated Zone: The area below the water table where all open spaces are filled with water under pressure equal to or greater than that of the atmosphere.

Saturation: The condition of a liquid when it has taken into solution the maximum possible quantity of a given substance at a given temperature and pressure.

Science Advisory Board (SAB): A group of external scientists who advise EPA on science and policy.

Scrap: Materials discarded from manufacturing operations that may be suitable for reprocessing.

Scrap Metal Processor: Intermediate operating facility where recovered metal is sorted, cleaned of contaminants, and prepared for recycling.

Screening: Use of screens to remove coarse floating and suspended solids from sewage.

Screening Risk Assessment: A risk assessment performed with few data and many assumptions to identify exposures that should be evaluated more carefully for potential risk.

Scrubber: An air pollution device that uses a spray of water or reactant or a dry process to trap pollutants in emissions.

Secondary Drinking Water Regulations: Non-enforceable regulations applying to public water systems and specifying the maximum contamination levels that, in the judgment of EPA, are required to protect the public welfare. These regulations apply to any contaminants that may adversely affect the odor or appearance of such water and consequently may cause people served by the system to discontinue its use.

Secondary Effect: Action of a stressor on supporting components of the ecosystem, which in turn impact the ecological component of concern. (See: primary effect.)

Secondary Materials: Materials that have been manufactured and used at least once and are to be used again.

Secondary Standards: National ambient air quality standards designed to protect welfare, including effects on soils, water, crops, vegetation, man-made (anthropogenic) materials, animals, wildlife, weather, visibility, and climate; damage to property; transportation hazards; economic values, and personal comfort and well-being.

Secondary Treatment: The second step in most publicly owned waste treatment systems in which bacteria consume the organic parts of the waste. It is accomplished by bringing together waste, bacteria, and oxygen in trickling filters or in the activated sludge process. This treatment removes floating and settleable solids and about 90 percent of the oxygen-demanding substances and suspended solids. Disinfection is the final stage of secondary treatment. (See: primary, tertiary treatment.)

Secure Chemical Landfill: (See:landfills.)

Secure Maximum Contaminant Level: Maximum permissible level of a contaminant in water delivered to the free flowing outlet of the ultimate user, or of contamination resulting from corrosion of piping and plumbing caused by water quality.

Sediment: Topsoil, sand, and minerals washed from the land into water, usually after rain or snow melt.

Sediment Yield: The quantity of sediment arriving at a specific location.

Sedimentation: Letting solids settle out of wastewater by gravity during treatment.

Sedimentation Tanks: Wastewater tanks in which floating wastes are skimmed off and settled solids are removed for disposal.

Sediments: Soil, sand, and minerals washed from land into water, usually after rain. They pile up in reservoirs, rivers and harbors, destroying fish and wildlife habitat, and clouding the water so that sunlight cannot reach aquatic plants. Careless farming, mining, and building activities will expose sediment materials, allowing them to wash off the land after rainfall.

Seed Protectant: A chemical applied before planting to protect seeds and seedlings from disease or insects.

Seepage: Percolation of water through the soil from unlined canals, ditches, laterals, watercourses, or water storage facilities.

Selective Pesticide: A chemical designed to affect only certain types of pests, leaving other plants and animals unharmed.

Semi-Confined Aquifer: An aquifer partially confined by soil layers of low permeability through which recharge and discharge can still occur.

Semivolatile Organic Compounds: Organic compounds that volatilize slowly at standard temperature (20 degrees C and 1 atm pressure).

Senescence: The aging process. Sometimes used to describe lakes or other bodies of water in advanced stages of eutrophication. Also used to describe plants and animals.

Septic System: An on-site system designed to treat and dispose of domestic sewage. A typical septic system consists of tank that receives waste from a residence or business and a system of tile lines or a pit for disposal of the liquid effluent (sludge) that remains after decomposition of the solids by bacteria in the tank and must be pumped out periodically.

Septic Tank: An underground storage tank for wastes from homes not connected to a sewer line. Waste goes directly from the home to the tank. (See: septic system.)

Service Connector: The pipe that carries tap water from a public water main to a building.

Service Line Sample: A one-liter sample of water that has been standing for at least 6 hours in a service pipeline and is collected according to federal regulations.

Service Pipe: The pipeline extending from the water main to the building served or to the consumer's system.

Set-Back: Setting a thermometer to a lower temperature when the building is unoccupied to reduce consumption of heating energy. Also refers to setting the thermometer to a higher temperature during unoccupied periods in the cooling season.

Settleable Solids: Material heavy enough to sink to the bottom of a wastewater treatment tank.

Settling Chamber: A series of screens placed in the way of flue gases to slow the stream of air, thus helping gravity to pull particles into a collection device.

Settling Tank: A holding area for wastewater, where heavier particles sink to the bottom for removal and disposal.

Sewage: The waste and wastewater produced by residential and commercial sources and discharged into sewers.

Sewage Lagoon: (See: lagoon.)

Sewage Sludge: Sludge produced at a Publicly Owned Treatment Works, the disposal of which is regulated under the Clean Water Act.

Sewer: A channel or conduit that carries wastewater and storm-water runoff from the source to a treatment plant or receiving stream. "Sanitary" sewers carry household, industrial, and commercial waste. "Storm" sewers carry runoff from rain or snow. "Combined" sewers handle both.

Sewerage: The entire system of sewage collection, treatment, and disposal.

Shading Coefficient: The amount of the sun's heat transmitted through a given window compared with that of a standard 1/8-inch-thick single pane of glass under the same conditions.

Sharps: Hypodermic needles, syringes (with or without the attached needle), Pasteur pipettes, scalpel blades, blood vials, needles with attached tubing, and culture dishes used in animal or human patient care or treatment, or in medical, research or industrial laboratories. Also included are other types of broken or unbroken glassware that were in contact with infectious agents, such as used slides and cover slips, and unused hypodermic and suture needles, syringes, and scalpel blades.

Shock Load: The arrival at a water treatment plant of raw water containing unusual amounts of algae, colloidal matter. color, suspended solids, turbidity, or other pollutants.

Short-Circuiting: When some of the water in tanks or basins flows faster than the rest; may result in shorter contact, reaction, or settling times than calculated or presumed.

Sick Building Syndrome: Building whose occupants experience acute health and/or comfort effects that appear to be linked to time spent therein, but where no specific illness or cause can be identified. Complaints may be localized in a particular room or zone, or may spread throughout the building. (See: building-related illness.)

Signal: The volume or product-level change produced by a leak in a tank.

Signal Words: The words used on a pesticide label—Danger, Warning, Caution—to indicate level of toxicity.

Significant Deterioration: Pollution resulting from a new source in previously "clean" areas. (See: prevention of significant deterioration.)

Significant Municipal Facilities: Those publicly owned sewage treatment plants that discharge a million gallons per day or more and are therefore considered by states to have the potential to substantially affect the quality of receiving waters.

Significant Non-Compliance: (See significant violations.)

Significant Potential Source of Contamination: A facility or activity that stores, uses, or produces compounds with potential for significant contaminating impact if released into the source water of a public water supply.

Significant Violations: Violations by point source dischargers of sufficient magnitude or duration to be a regulatory priority.

Silt: Sedimentary materials composed of fine or intermediate-sized mineral particles.

Silviculture: Management of forest land for timber.

Single-Breath Canister: Small one-liter canister designed to capture a single breath. Used in air pollutant ingestion research.

Sink: Place in the environment where a compound or material collects.

Sinking: Controlling oil spills by using an agent to trap the oil and sink it to the bottom of the body of water where the agent and the oil are biodegraded.

SIP Call: EPA action requiring a state to resubmit all or part of its State Implementation Plan to demonstrate attainment of the require national ambient air quality standards within the statutory deadline. A SIP Revision is a revision of a SIP altered at the request of EPA or on a state's initiative. (See: State Implementation Plan.)

Site: An area or place within the jurisdiction of the EPA and/or a state.

Site Assessment Program: A means of evaluating hazardous waste sites through preliminary assessments and site inspections to develop a Hazard Ranking System score.

Site Inspection: The collection of information from a Superfund site to determine the extent and severity of hazards posed by the site. It follows and is more extensive than a preliminary assessment. The purpose is to gather information necessary to score the site, using the Hazard Ranking System, and to determine if it presents an immediate threat requiring prompt removal.

Site Safety Plan: A crucial element in all removal actions, it includes information on equipment being used, precautions to be taken, and steps to take in the event of an on-site emergency.

Siting: The process of choosing a location for a facility.

Skimming: Using a machine to remove oil or scum from the surface of the water.

Slow Sand Filtration: Passage of raw water through a bed of sand at low velocity, resulting in substantial removal of chemical and biological contaminants.

Sludge: A semi-solid residue from any of a number of air or water treatment processes; can be a hazardous waste.

Sludge Digester: Tank in which complex organic substances like sewage sludges are biologically dredged. During these reactions, energy is released and much of the sewage is converted to methane, carbon dioxide, and water.

Slurry: A watery mixture of insoluble matter resulting from some pollution control techniques.

Small Quantity Generator (SQG-sometimes referred to as "Squeegee"): Persons or enterprises that produce 220-2200 pounds per month of hazardous waste; they are required to keep more records than conditionally exempt generators. The largest category of hazardous waste generators, SQGs, include automotive shops, dry cleaners, photographic developers, and many other small businesses. (See: conditionally exempt generators.)

Smelter: A facility that melts or fuses ore, often with an accompanying chemical change, to separate its metal content. Emissions cause pollution. "Smelting" is the process involved.

Smog: Air pollution typically associated with oxidants. (See: photochemical smog.)

Smoke: Particles suspended in air after incomplete combustion.

Soft Detergents: Cleaning agents that break down in nature.

Soft Water: Any water that does not contain a significant amount of dissolved minerals such as salts of calcium or magnesium.

Soil Adsorption Field: A sub-surface area containing a trench or bed with clean stones and a system of piping through which treated sewage may seep into the surrounding soil for further treatment and disposal.

Soil and Water Conservation Practices: Control measures consisting of managerial, vegetative, and structural practices to reduce the loss of soil and water.

Soil Conditioner: An organic material like humus or compost that helps soil absorb water, build a bacterial community, and take up mineral nutrients.

Soil Erodibility: An indicator of a soil's susceptibility to raindrop impact, runoff, and other erosive processes.

Soil Gas: Gaseous elements and compounds in the small spaces between particles of the earth and soil. Such gases can be moved or driven out under pressure.

Soil Moisture: The water contained in the pore space of the unsaturated zone.

Soil Sterilant: A chemical that temporarily or permanently prevents the growth of all plants and animals.

Solder: Metallic compound used to seal joints between pipes. Until recently, most solder contained 50 percent lead. Use of solder containing more than 0.2 percent lead in pipes carrying drinking water is now prohibited.

Sole-Source Aquifer: An aquifer that supplies 50-percent or more of the drinking water of an area.

Solid Waste: Non-liquid, non-soluble materials ranging from municipal garbage to industrial wastes that contain complex and sometimes hazardous substances. Solid wastes also include sewage sludge, agricultural refuse, demolition wastes, and mining residues. Technically, solid waste also refers to liquids and gases in containers.

Solid Waste Disposal: The final placement of refuse that is not salvaged or recycled.

Solid Waste Management: Supervised handling of waste materials from their source through recovery processes to disposal.

Solidification and Stabilization: Removal of wastewater from a waste or changing it chemically to make it less permeable and susceptible to transport by water.

Solubility: The amount of mass of a compound that will dissolve in a unit volume of solution. Aqueous Solubility is the maximum concentration of a chemical that will dissolve in pure water at a reference temperature.

Soot: Carbon dust formed by incomplete combustion.

Sorption: The action of soaking up or attracting substances; process used in many pollution control systems.

Source Area: The location of liquid hydrocarbons or the zone of highest soil or groundwater concentrations, or both, of the chemical of concern.

Source Characterization Measurements: Measurements made to estimate the rate of release of pollutants into the environment from a source such as an incinerator, landfill, etc.

Source Reduction: Reducing the amount of materials entering the waste stream from a specific source by redesigning products or patterns of production or consumption (*e.g.*, using returnable beverage containers). Synonymous with waste reduction.

Source Separation: Segregating various wastes at the point of generation (*e.g.*, separation of paper, metal and glass from other wastes to make recycling simpler and more efficient).

Source-Water Protection Area: The area delineated by a state for a Public Water Supply or including numerous such suppliers, whether the source is ground water or surface water or both.

Sparge or Sparging: Injection of air below the water table to strip dissolved volatile organic compounds and/or oxygenate ground water to facilitate aerobic biodegradation of organic compounds.

Special Local-Needs Registration: Registration of a pesticide product by a state agency for a specific use that is not federally registered. However, the active ingredient must be federally registered for other uses. The special use is specific to that state and is often minor, thus may not warrant the additional cost of a full federal registration process. SLN registration cannot be issued for new active ingredients, food-use active ingredients without tolerances, or for a canceled registration. The products cannot be shipped across state lines.

Special Review: Formerly known as Rebuttable Presumption Against Registration (RPAR), this is the regulatory process through which existing pesticides suspected of posing unreasonable risks to human health, non-target organisms, or the environment are referred for review by EPA. Such review requires an intensive risk/benefit analysis with opportunity for public comment. If risk is found to outweigh social and economic benefits, regulatory actions can be initiated, ranging from label revisions and use-restriction to cancellation or suspended registration.

Special Waste: Items such as household hazardous waste, bulky wastes (refrigerators, pieces of furniture, etc.) tires, and used oil.

Species: 1. A reproductively isolated aggregate of interbreeding organisms having common attributes and usually designated by a common name. 2. An organism belonging to belonging to such a category.

Specific Conductance: Rapid method of estimating the dissolved solid content of a water supply by testing its capacity to carry an electrical current.

Specific Yield: The amount of water a unit volume of saturated permeable rock will yield when drained by gravity.

Spill Prevention, Containment, and Countermeasures Plan (SPCP): Plan covering the release of hazardous substances as defined in the Clean Water Act.

Spoil: Dirt or rock removed from its original location—destroying the composition of the soil in the process—as in strip-mining, dredging, or construction.

Sprawl: Unplanned development of open land.

Spray Tower Scrubber: A device that sprays alkaline water into a chamber where acid gases are present to aid in neutralizing the gas.

Spring: Ground water seeping out of the earth where the water table intersects the ground surface.

Spring Melt/Thaw: The process whereby warm temperatures melt winter snow and ice. Because various forms of acid deposition may have been stored in the frozen water, the melt can result in abnormally large amounts of acidity entering streams and rivers, sometimes causing fish kills.

Stabilization: Conversion of the active organic matter in sludge into inert, harmless material.

Stabilization Ponds: (See: lagoon.)

Stable Air: A motionless mass of air that holds, instead of dispersing, pollutants.

Stack: A chimney, smokestack, or vertical pipe that discharges used air.

Stack Effect: Air, as in a chimney, that moves upward because it is warmer than the ambient atmosphere.

Stack Effect: Flow of air resulting from warm air rising, creating a positive pressure area at the top of a building and negative pressure area at the bottom. This effect can overpower the mechanical system and disrupt building ventilation and air circulation.

Stack Gas: (See: flue gas.)

Stage II Controls: Systems placed on service station gasoline pumps to control and capture gasoline vapors during refuelling.

Stagnation: Lack of motion in a mass of air or water that holds pollutants in place.

Stakeholder: Any organization, governmental entity, or individual that has a stake in or may be impacted by a given approach to environmental regulation, pollution prevention, energy conservation, etc.

Standard Industrial Classification Code: Also known as SIC Codes, a method of grouping industries with similar products or services and assigning codes to these groups.

Standard Sample: The part of finished drinking water that is examined for the presence of coliform bacteria.

Standards: Norms that impose limits on the amount of pollutants or emissions produced. EPA establishes minimum standards, but states are allowed to be stricter.

Start of a Response Action: The point in time when there is a guarantee or set-aside of funding by EPA, other federal agencies, states or Principal Responsible Parties in order to begin response actions at a Superfund site.

State Emergency Response Commission (SERC): Commission appointed by each state governor according to the requirements of SARA Title III. The SERCs designate emergency planning districts, appoint local emergency planning committees, and supervise and coordinate their activities.

State Environmental Goals and Indication Project: Program to assist state environmental agencies by providing technical and financial assistance in the development of environmental goals and indicators.

State Implementation Plans (SIP): EPA approved state plans for the establishment, regulation, and enforcement of air pollution standards.

State Management Plan: Under FIFRA, a state management plan required by EPA to allow states, tribes, and U.S. territories the flexibility to design and implement ways to protect ground water from the use of certain pesticides.

Static Water Depth: The vertical distance from the centerline of the pump discharge down to the surface level of the free pool while no water is being drawn from the pool or water table.

Static Water Level: 1. Elevation or level of the water table in a well when the pump is not operating. 2. The level or elevation to which water would rise in a tube connected to an artesian aquifer or basin in a conduit under pressure.

Stationary Source: A fixed-site producer of pollution, mainly power plants and other facilities using industrial combustion processes.

Sterilization: The removal or destruction of all microorganisms, including pathogenic and other bacteria, vegetative forms, and spores.

Sterilizer: One of three groups of anti-microbials registered by EPA for public health uses. EPA considers an antimicrobial to be a sterilizer when it destroys or eliminates all forms of bacteria, viruses, and fungi and their spores. Because spores are considered the most difficult form of microorganism to destroy, EPA considers the term sporicide to be synonymous with sterilizer.

Storage: Temporary holding of waste pending treatment or disposal, as in containers, tanks, waste piles, and surface impoundments.

Storm Sewer: A system of pipes (separate from sanitary sewers) that carries water runoff from buildings and land surfaces.

Stratification: Separating into layers.

Stratigraphy: Study of the formation, composition, and sequence of sediments, whether consolidated or not.

Stratosphere: The portion of the atmosphere 10-to-25 miles above the earth's surface.

Stressors: Physical, chemical, or biological entities that can induce adverse effects on ecosystems or human health.

Strip-Cropping: Growing crops in a systematic arrangement of strips or bands that serve as barriers to wind and water erosion.

Strip-Mining: A process that uses machines to scrape soil or rock away from mineral deposits just under the earth's surface.

Structural Deformation: Distortion in walls of a tank after liquid has been added or removed.

Subchronic: Of intermediate duration, usually used to describe studies or periods of exposure lasting between 5 and 90 days.

Subchronic Exposure: Multiple or continuous exposures lasting for approximately ten percent of an experimental species lifetime, usually over a three-month period.

Submerged Aquatic Vegetation: Vegetation that lives at or below the water surface; an important habitat for young fish and other aquatic organisms.

Subwatershed: Topographic perimeter of the catchment area of a stream tributary.

Sulfur Dioxide (SO_2): A pungent, colorless, gasformed primarily by the combustion of fossil fuels; becomes a pollutant when present in large amounts.

Sump: A pit or tank that catches liquid runoff for drainage or disposal.

Superchlorination: Chlorination with doses that are deliberately selected to produce water free of combined residuals so large as to require dechlorination.

Supercritical Water: A type of thermal treatment using moderate temperatures and high pressures to enhance the ability of water to break down large organic molecules into smaller, less toxic ones. Oxygen injected during this process combines with simple organic compounds to form carbon dioxide and water.

Superfund: The program operated under the legislative authority of CERCLA and SARA that funds and carries out EPA solid waste emergency and long-term removal and remedial activities. These activities include establishing the National Priorities List, investigating sites for inclusion on the list, determining their priority, and conducting and/or supervising cleanup and other remedial actions.

Superfund Innovative Technology Evaluation (SITE) Program: EPA program to promote development and use of innovative treatment and site characterization technologies in Superfund site cleanups.

Supplemental Registration: An arrangement whereby a registrant licenses another company to market its pesticide product under the second company's registration.

Supplier of Water: Any person who owns or operates a public water supply.

Surface Impoundment: Treatment, storage, or disposal of liquid hazardous wastes in ponds.

Surface Runoff: Precipitation, snow melt, or irrigation water in excess of what can infiltrate the soil surface and be stored in small surface depressions; a major transporter of non-point source pollutants in rivers, streams, and lakes.

Surface Uranium Mines: Strip mining operations for removal of uranium-bearing ore.

Surface Water: All water naturally open to the atmosphere (rivers, lakes, reservoirs, ponds, streams, impoundments, seas, estuaries, etc.)

Surface-Water Treatment Rule: Rule that specifies maximum contaminant level goals for Giardia lamblia, viruses, and Legionella and promulgates filtration and disinfection requirements for public water systems using surface-water or ground-water sources under the direct influence of surface water. The regulations also specify water quality, treatment, and watershed protection criteria under which filtration may be avoided.

Surfacing ACM: Asbestos-containing material that is sprayed or troweled on or otherwise applied to surfaces, such as acoustical plaster on ceilings and fireproofing materials on structural members.

Surfacing Material: Material sprayed or troweled onto structural members (beams, columns, or decking) for fire protection; or on ceilings or walls for fireproofing, acoustical or decorative purposes. Includes textured plaster, and other textured wall and ceiling surfaces.

Surfactant: A detergent compound that promotes lathering.

Surrogate Data: Data from studies of test organisms or a test substance that are used to estimate the characteristics or effects on another organism or substance.

Surveillance System: A series of monitoring devices designed to check on environmental conditions.

Susceptibility Analysis: An analysis to determine whether a Public Water Supply is subject to significant pollution from known potential sources.

Suspect Material: Building material suspected of containing asbestos; *e.g.*, surfacing material, floor tile, ceiling tile, thermal system insulation.

Suspended Loads: Specific sediment particles maintained in the water column by turbulence and carried with the flow of water.

Suspended Solids: Small particles of solid pollutants that float on the surface of, or are suspended in, sewage or other liquids. They resist removal by conventional means.

Suspension: Suspending the use of a pesticide when EPA deems it necessary to prevent an imminent hazard resulting from its continued use. An emergency suspension takes effect immediately; under an ordinary suspension a registrant can request a hearing before the suspension goes into effect. Such a hearing process might take six months.

Suspension Culture: Cells growing in a liquid nutrient medium.

Swamp: A type of wetland dominated by woody vegetation but without appreciable peat deposits. Swamps may be fresh or salt water and tidal or non-tidal. (See: wetlands.)

Synergism: An interaction of two or more chemicals that results in an effect greater than the sum of their separate effects.

Synthetic Organic Chemicals (SOCs): Man-made (anthropogenic) organic chemicals. Some SOCs are volatile; others tend to stay dissolved in water instead of evaporating.

System With a Single Service Connection: A system that supplies drinking water to consumers via a single service line.

Systemic Pesticide: A chemical absorbed by an organism that interacts with the organism and makes the organism toxic to pests.

T

Tail Water: The runoff of irrigation water from the lower end of an irrigated field.

Tailings: Residue of raw material or waste separated out during the processing of crops or mineral ores.

Tailpipe Standards: Emissions limitations applicable to mobile source engine exhausts.

Tampering: Adjusting, negating, or removing pollution control equipment on a motor vehicle.

Technical Assistance Grant (TAG): As part of the Superfund program, Technical Assistance Grants of up to $50,000 are provided to citizens' groups to obtain assistance in interpreting information related to clean-ups at Superfund sites or those proposed for the National Priorities List. Grants are used by such groups to hire technical advisors to help them understand the site-related technical information for the duration of response activities.

Technical-Grade Active Ingredient (TGA): A pesticide chemical in pure form as it is manufactured prior to being formulated into an end-use product (*e.g.* wettable powders, granules, emulsifiable concentrates). Registered manufactured products composed of such chemicals are known as Technical Grade Products.

Technology-Based Limitations: Industry-specific effluent limitations based on best available preventive technology applied to a discharge when it will not cause a violation of water quality standards at low stream flows. Usually applied to discharges into large rivers.

Technology-Based Standards: Industry-specific effluent limitations applicable to direct and indirect sources which are developed on a category-by-category basis using statutory factors, not including water-quality effects.

Teratogen: A substance capable of causing birth defects.

Teratogenesis: The introduction of nonhereditary birth defects in a developing fetus by exogenous factors such as physical or chemical agents acting in the womb to interfere with normal embryonic development.

Terracing: Dikes built along the contour of sloping farm land that hold runoff and sediment to reduce erosion.

Tertiary Treatment: Advanced cleaning of wastewater that goes beyond the secondary or biological stage, removing nutrients such as phosphorus, nitrogen, and most BOD and suspended solids.

Theoretical Maximum Residue Contribution: The theoretical maximum amount of a pesticide in the daily diet of an average person. It assumes that the diet is composed of all food items for which there are tolerance-level residues of the pesticide. The TMRC is expressed as milligrams of pesticide/kilograms of body weight/day.

Therapeutic Index: The ratio of the dose required to produce toxic or lethal effects to the dose required to produce non adverse or therapeutic response.

Thermal Pollution: Discharge of heated water from industrial processes that can kill or injure aquatic organisms.

Thermal Stratification: The formation of layers of different temperatures in a lake or reservoir.

Thermal System Insulation (TSI): Asbestos-containing material applied to pipes, fittings, boilers, breeching, tanks, ducts, or other interior structural components to prevent heat loss or gain or water condensation.

Thermal Treatment: Use of elevated temperatures to treat hazardous wastes. (See: incineration; pyrolysis.)

Thermocline: The middle layer of a thermally stratified lake or reservoir. In this layer, there is a rapid decrease in temperatures in a lake or reservoir.

Threshold: The lowest dose of a chemical at which a specified measurable effect is observed and below which it is not observed.

Threshold Level: Time-weighted average pollutant concentration values, exposure beyond which is likely to adversely affect human health. (See: environmental exposure)

Threshold Limit Value (TLV): The concentration of an airborne substance to which an average person can be repeatedly exposed without adverse effects. TLVs may be expressed in three ways: (1) TLV-TWA—Time weighted average, based on an allowable exposure averaged over a normal 8-hour workday or 40-hour work- week; (2) TLV-STEL—Short-term exposure limit or maximum concentration for a brief specified period of time, depending on a specific chemical (TWA must still be met); and (3) TLV-C—Ceiling Exposure Limit or maximum exposure concentration not to be exceeded under any circumstances. (TWA must still be met.)

Threshold Odor: (See: Odor threshold)

Threshold Planning Quantity: A quantity designated for each chemical on the list of extremely hazardous substances that triggers notification by facilities to the State Emergency Response Commission that such facilities are subject to emergency planning requirements under SARA Title III.

Thropic Levels: A functional classification of species that is based on feeding relationships (*e.g.* generally aquatic and terrestrial green plants comprise the first thropic level, and herbivores comprise the second.)

Tidal Marsh: Low, flat marshlands traversed by channels and tidal hollows, subject to tidal inundation; normally, the only vegetation present is salt-tolerant bushes and grasses. (See: wetlands.)

Tillage: Plowing, seedbed preparation, and cultivation practices.

Time-weighted Average (TWA): In air sampling, the average air concentration of contaminants during a given period.

Tire Processor: Intermediate operating facility where recovered tires are processed in preparation for recycling.

Tires: As used in recycling, passenger car and truck tires (excludes airplane, bus, motorcycle and special service military, agricultural, off-the-road and-slow speed industrial tires). Car and truck tires are recycled into rubber products such as trash cans, storage containers, rubberized asphalt or used whole for playground and reef construction.

Tolerance Petition: A formal request to establish a new tolerance or modify an existing one.

Tolerances: Permissible residue levels for pesticides in raw agricultural produce and processed foods. Whenever a pesticide is registered for use on a food or a feed crop, a tolerance (or exemption from the tolerance requirement) must be established. EPA establishes the tolerance levels, which are enforced by the Food and Drug Administration and the Department of Agriculture.

Tonnage: The amount of waste that a landfill accepts, usually expressed in tons per month. The rate at which a landfill accepts waste is limited by the landfill's permit.

Topography: The physical features of a surface area including relative elevations and the position of natural and man-made (anthropogenic) features.

Total Dissolved Phosphorous: The total phosphorous content of all material that will pass through a filter, which is determined as orthophosphate without prior digestion or hydrolysis. Also called soluble P. or ortho P.

Total Dissolved Solids (TDS): All material that passes the standard glass river filter; now called total filtrable residue. Term is used to reflect salinity.

Total Maximum Daily Load (TMDL): A calculation of the highest amount of a pollutant that a water body can receive and safely meet water quality standards set by the state, territory, or authorized tribe.

Total Petroleum Hydrocarbons (TPH): Measure of the concentration or mass of petroleum hydrocarbon constituents present in a given amount of soil or water. The word "total" is a misnomer-few, if any, of the procedures for quantifying hydrocarbons can measure all of them in a given sample. Volatile ones are usually lost in the process and not quantified and non-petroleum hydrocarbons sometimes appear in the analysis.

Total Recovered Petroleum Hydrocarbon: A method for measuring petroleum hydrocarbons in samples of soil or water.

Total Suspended Particles (TSP): A method of monitoring airborne particulate matter by total weight.

Total Suspended Solids (TSS): A measure of the suspended solids in wastewater, effluent, or water bodies, determined by tests for "total suspended non-filterable solids." (See: suspended solids.)

Toxaphene: Chemical that causes adverse health effects in domestic water supplies and is toxic to fresh water and marine aquatic life.

Toxic Chemical: Any chemical listed in EPA rules as "Toxic Chemicals Subject to Section 313 of the Emergency Planning and Community Right-to-Know Act of 1986."

Toxic Chemical Release Form: Information form required of facilities that manufacture, process, or use (in quantities above a specific amount) chemicals listed under SARA Title III.

Toxic Chemical Use Substitution: Replacing toxic chemicals with less harmful chemicals in industrial processes.

Toxic Cloud: Airborne plume of gases, vapors, fumes, or aerosols containing toxic materials.

Toxic Concentration: The concentration at which a substance produces a toxic effect.

Toxic Dose: The dose level at which a substance produces a toxic effect.

Toxic Pollutants: Materials that cause death, disease, or birth defects in organisms that ingest or absorb them. The quantities and exposures necessary to cause these effects can vary widely.

Toxic Release Inventory: Database of toxic releases in the United States compiled from SARA Title III Section 313 reports.

Toxic Substance: A chemical or mixture that may present an unreasonable risk of injury to health or the environment.

Toxic Waste: A waste that can produce injury if inhaled, swallowed, or absorbed through the skin.

Toxicant: A harmful substance or agent that may injure an exposed organism.

Toxicity: The degree to which a substance or mixture of substances can harm humans or animals. *Acute toxicity* involves harmful effects in an organism through a single or short-term exposure. *Chronic toxicity* is the ability of a substance or mixture of substances to cause harmful effects over an extended period, usually upon repeated or continuous exposure sometimes lasting for the entire life of the exposed organism. *Subchronic toxicity* is the ability of the substance to cause effects for more than one year but less than the lifetime of the exposed organism.

Toxicity Assessment: Characterization of the toxicological properties and effects of a chemical, with special emphasis on establishment of dose-response characteristics.

Toxicity Testing: Biological testing (usually with an invertebrate, fish, or small mammal) to determine the adverse effects of a compound or effluent.

Toxicological Profile: An examination, summary, and interpretation of a hazardous substance to determine levels of exposure and associated health effects.

Transboundary Pollutants: Air pollution that travels from one jurisdiction to another, often crossing state or international boundaries. Also applies to water pollution.

Transfer Station: Facility where solid waste is transferred from collection vehicles to larger trucks or rail cars for longer distance transport.

Transient Water System: A non-community water system that does not serve 25 of the same nonresidents per day for more than six months per year.

Transmission Lines: Pipelines that transport raw water from its source to a water treatment plant, then to the distribution grid system.

Transmissivity: The ability of an aquifer to transmit water.

Transpiration: The process by which water vapor is lost to the atmosphere from living plants. The term can also be applied to the quantity of water thus dissipated.

Transportation Control Measures (TCMs): Steps taken by a locality to reduce vehicular emission and improve air quality by reducing or changing the flow of traffic; *e.g.* bus and HOV lanes, carpooling and other forms of ride-shairing, public transit, bicycle lanes.

Transporter: Hauling firm that picks up properly packaged and labeled hazardous waste from generators and transports it to designated facilities for treatment, storage, or disposal. Transporters are subject to EPA and DOT hazardous waste regulations.

Trash: Material considered worthless or offensive that is thrown away. Generally defined as dry waste material, but in common usage it is a synonym for garbage, rubbish, or refuse.

Trash-to-Energy Plan: Burning trash to produce energy.

Treatability Studies: Tests of potential cleanup technologies conducted in a laboratory (See: benchscale tests.)

Treated Regulated Medical Waste: Medical waste treated to substantially reduce or eliminate its pathogenicity, but that has not yet been destroyed.

Treated Wastewater: Wastewater that has been subjected to one or more physical, chemical, and biological processes to reduce its potential of being health hazard.

Treatment: 1. Any method, technique, or process designed to remove solids and/or pollutants from solid waste, waste-streams, effluents, and air emissions. 2. Methods used to change the biological character or composition of any regulated medical waste so as to substantially reduce or eliminate its potential for causing disease.

Treatment Plant: A structure built to treat wastewater before discharging it into the environment.

Treatment, Storage, and Disposal Facility: Site where a hazardous substance is treated, stored, or disposed of. TSD facilities are regulated by EPA and states under RCRA.

Tremie: Device used to place concrete or grout under water.

Trial Burn: An incinerator test in which emissions are monitored for the presence of specific organic compounds, particulates, and hydrogen chloride.

Trichloroethylene (TCE): A stable, low boiling-point colorless liquid, toxic if inhaled. Used as a solvent or metal degreasing agent, and in other industrial applications.

Trickle Irrigation: Method in which water drips to the soil from perforated tubes or emitters.

Trickling Filter: A coarse treatment system in which wastewater is trickled over a bed of stones or other material covered with bacteria that break down the organic waste and produce clean water.

Trihalomethane (THM): One of a family of organic compounds named as derivative of methane. THMs are generally by-products of chlorination of drinking water that contains organic material.

Troposhpere: The layer of the atmosphere closest to the earth's surface.

Trust Fund (CERCLA): A fund set up under the Comprehensive Environmental Response, Compensation and Liability Act (CERCLA) to help pay for cleanup of hazardous waste sites and for legal action to force those responsible for the sites to clean them up.

Tube Settler: Device using bundles of tubes to let solids in water settle to the bottom for removal by conventional sludge collection means; sometimes used in sedimentation basins and clarifiers to improve particle removal.

Tuberculation: Development or formation of small mounds of corrosion products on the inside of iron pipe. These tubercules roughen the inside of the pipe, increasing its resistance to water flow.

Tundra: A type of treeless ecosystem dominated by lichens, mosses, grasses, and woody plants. Tundra is found at high latitudes (arctic tundra) and high altitudes (alpine tundra). Arctic tundra is underlain by permafrost and is usually water saturated. (See: wetlands.)

Turbidimeter: A device that measures the cloudiness of suspended solids in a liquid; a measure of the quantity of suspended solids.

Turbidity: 1. Haziness in air caused by the presence of particles and pollutants. 2. A cloudy condition in water due to suspended silt or organic matter.

U

Ultra Clean Coal (UCC): Coal that is washed, ground into fine particles, then chemically treated to remove sulfur, ash, silicone, and other substances; usually briquetted and coated with a sealant made from coal.

Ultraviolet Rays: Radiation from the sun that can be useful or potentially harmful. UV rays from one part of the spectrum (UV-A) enhance plant life. UV rays from other parts of the spectrum (UV-B) can cause skin cancer or other tissue damage. The ozone layer in the atmosphere partly shields us from ultraviolet rays reaching the earth's surface.

Uncertainty Factor: One of several factors used in calculating the reference dose from experimental data. UFs are intended to account for (1) the variation in sensitivity among humans; (2) the uncertainty in extrapolating animal data to humans; (3) the uncertainty in extrapolating data obtained in a study that covers less than the full life of the exposed animal or human; and (4) the uncertainty in using LOAEL data rather than NOAEL data.

Unconfined Aquifer: An aquifer containing water that is not under pressure; the water level in a well is the same as the water table outside the well.

Underground Injection Control (UIC): The program under the Safe Drinking Water Act that regulates the use of wells to pump fluids into the ground.

Underground Injection Wells: Steel- and concrete-encased shafts into which hazardous waste is deposited by force and under pressure.

Underground Sources of Drinking Water: Aquifers currently being used as a source of drinking water or those capable of supplying a public water system. They have a total dissolved solids content of 10,000 milligrams per liter or less, and are not "exempted aquifers." (See: exempted aquifer.)

Underground Storage Tank (UST): A tank located at least partially underground and designed to hold gasoline or other petroleum products or chemicals.

Unreasonable Risk: Under the Federal Insecticide, Fungicide, and Rodenticide Act (FIFRA), "unreasonable adverse effects" means any unreasonable risk to man or the environment, taking into account the medical, economic, social, and environmental costs and benefits of any pesticide.

Unsaturated Zone: The area above the water table where soil pores are not fully saturated, although some water may be present.

Uranium Mill Tailings Piles: Former uranium ore processing sites that contain leftover radioactive materials (wastes), including radium and unrecovered uranium.

Uranium Mill-Tailings Waste Piles: Licensed active mills with tailings piles and evaporation ponds created by acid or alkaline leaching processes.

Urban Runoff: Storm water from city streets and adjacent domestic or commercial properties that carries pollutants of various kinds into the sewer systems and receiving waters.

Urea-Formaldehyde Foam Insulation: A material once used to conserve energy by sealing crawl spaces, attics, etc.; no longer used because emissions were found to be a health hazard.

Use Cluster: A set of competing chemicals, processes, and/or technologies that can substitute for one another in performing a particular function.

Used Oil: Spent motor oil from passenger cars and trucks collected at specified locations for recycling (not included in the category of municipal solid waste).

User Fee: Fee collected from only those persons who use a particular service, as compared to one collected from the public in general.

Utility Load: The total electricity demand for a utility district.

V

Vadose Zone: The zone between land surface and the water table within which the moisture content is less than saturation (except in the capillary fringe) and pressure is less than atmospheric. Soil pore space also typically contains air or other gases. The capillary fringe is included in the vadose zone. (See: Unsaturated Zone.)

Valued Environmental Attributes/Components: Those aspects(components/processes/functions) of ecosystems, human health, and environmental welfare considered to be important and potentially at risk from human activity or natural hazards. Similar to the term "valued environmental components" used in environmental impact assessment.

Vapor: The gas given off by substances that are solids or liquids at ordinary atmospheric pressure and temperatures.

Vapor Capture System: Any combination of hoods and ventilation system that captures or contains organic vapors so they may be directed to an abatement or recovery device.

Vapor Dispersion: The movement of vapor clouds in air due to wind, thermal action, gravity spreading, and mixing.

Vapor Plumes: Flue gases visible because they contain water droplets.

Vapor Pressure: A measure of a substance's propensity to evaporate, vapor pressure is the force per unit area exerted by vapor in an equilibrium state with surroundings at a given pressure. It increases exponentially with an increase in temperature. A relative measure of chemical volatility, vapor pressure is used to calculate water partition coefficients and volatilization rate constants.

Vapor Recovery System: A system by which the volatile gases from gasoline are captured instead of being released into the atmosphere.

Variance: Government permission for a delay or exception in the application of a given law, ordinance, or regulation.

Vector: 1. An organism, often an insect or rodent, that carries disease. 2. Plasmids, viruses, or bacteria used to transport genes into a host cell. A gene is placed in the vector; the vector then "infects" the bacterium.

Vegetative Controls: Non-point source pollution control practices that involve vegetative cover to reduce erosion and minimize loss of pollutants.

Vehicle Miles Travelled (VMT): A measure of the extent of motor vehicle operation; the total number of vehicle miles travelled within a specific geographic area over a given period of time.

Ventilation Rate: The rate at which indoor air enters and leaves a building. Expressed as the number of changes of outdoor air per unit of time (air changes per hour (ACH), or the rate at which a volume of outdoor air enters in cubic feet per minute (CFM).

Ventilation/Suction: The act of admitting fresh air into a space in order to replace stale or contaminated air; achieved by blowing air into the space. Similarly, suction represents the admission of fresh air into an interior space by lowering the pressure outside of the space, thereby drawing the contaminated air outward.

Venturi Scrubbers: Air pollution control devices that use water to remove particulate matter from emissions.

Vinyl Chloride: A chemical compound, used in producing some plastics, that is believed to be oncogenic.

Virgin Materials: Resources extracted from nature in their raw form, such as timber or metal ore.

Viscosity: The molecular friction within a fluid that produces flow resistance.

Volatile: Any substance that evaporates readily.

Volatile Liquids: Liquids which easily vaporize or evaporate at room temperature.

Volatile Organic Compound (VOC): Any organic compound that participates in atmospheric photochemical reactions except those designated by EPA as having negligible photochemical reactivity.

Volatile Solids: Those solids in water or other liquids that are lost on ignition of the dry solids at 550° centigrade.

Volatile Synthetic Organic Chemicals: Chemicals that tend to volatilize or evaporate.

Volume Reduction: Processing waste materials to decrease the amount of space they occupy, usually by compacting, shredding, incineration, or composting.

Volumetric Tank Test: One of several tests to determine the physical integrity of a storage tank; the volume of fluid in the tank is measured directly or calculated from product-level changes. A marked drop in volume indicates a leak.

Vulnerability Analysis: Assessment of elements in the community that are susceptible to damage if hazardous materials are released.

Vulnerable Zone: An area over which the airborne concentration of a chemical accidentally released could reach the level of concern.

W

Waste: 1. Unwanted materials left over from a manufacturing process. 2. Refuse from places of human or animal habitation.

Waste Characterization: Identification of chemical and microbiological constituents of a waste material.

Waste Exchange: Arrangement in which companies exchange their wastes for the benefit of both parties.

Waste Feed: The continuous or intermittent flow of wastes into an incinerator.

Waste Generation: The weight or volume of materials and products that enter the waste stream before recycling, composting, landfilling, or combustion takes place. Also can represent the amount of waste generated by a given source or category of sources.

Waste Load Allocation: 1. The maximum load of pollutants each discharger of waste is allowed to release into a particular waterway. Discharge limits are usually required for each specific water quality criterion being, or expected to be, violated. 2. The portion of a stream's total assimilative capacity assigned to an individual discharge.

Waste Minimization: Measures or techniques that reduce the amount of wastes generated during industrial production processes; term is also applied to recycling and other efforts to reduce the amount of waste going into the waste stream.

Waste Piles: Non-containerized, lined or unlined accumulations of solid, nonflowing waste.

Waste Reduction: Using source reduction, recycling, or composting to prevent or reduce waste generation.

Waste Stream: The total flow of solid waste from homes, businesses, institutions, and manufacturing plants that is recycled, burned, or disposed of in landfills, or segments thereof such as the "residential waste stream" or the "recyclable waste stream."

Waste Treatment Lagoon: Impoundment made by excavation or earth fill for biological treatment of wastewater.

Waste Treatment Plant: A facility containing a series of tanks, screens, filters and other processes by which pollutants are removed from water.

Waste Treatment Stream: The continuous movement of waste from generator to treater and disposer.

Waste-Heat Recovery: Recovering heat discharged as a byproduct of one process to provide heat needed by a second process.

Waste-to-Energy Facility/Municipal-Waste Combustor: Facility where recovered municipal solid waste is converted into a usable form of energy, usually via combustion.

Wastewater: The spent or used water from a home, community, farm, or industry that contains dissolved or suspended matter. Water Pollution: The presence in water of enough harmful or objectionable material to damage the water's quality.

Wastewater Infrastructure: The plan or network for the collection, treatment, and disposal of sewage in a community. The level of treatment will depend on the size of the community, the type of discharge, and/or the designated use of the receiving water.

Wastewater Operations and Maintenance: Actions taken after construction to ensure that facilities constructed to treat wastewater will be operated, maintained, and managed to reach prescribed effluent levels in an optimum manner.

Wastewater Treatment Plan: A facility containing a series of tanks, screens, filters, and other processes by which pollutants are removed from water. Most treatments include chlorination to attain safe drinking water standards.

Water Purveyor: A public utility, mutual water company, county water district, or municipality that delivers drinking water to customers.

Water Quality Criteria: Levels of water quality expected to render a body of water suitable for its designated use. Criteria are based on specific levels of pollutants that would make the water harmful if used for drinking, swimming, farming, fish production, or industrial processes.

Water Quality Standards: State-adopted and EPA-approved ambient standards for water bodies. The standards prescribe the use of the water body and establish the water quality criteria that must be met to protect designated uses.

Water Quality-Based Limitations: Effluent limitations applied to dischargers when mere technology-based limitations would cause violations of water quality standards. Usually applied to discharges into small streams.

Water Quality-Based Permit: A permit with an effluent limit more stringent than one based on technology performance. Such limits may be necessary to protect the designated use of receiving waters (*e.g.* recreation, irrigation, industry or water supply).

Water Solubility: The maximum possible concentration of a chemical compound dissolved in water. If a substance is water soluble it can very readily disperse through the environment.

Water Storage Pond: An impound for liquid wastes designed to accomplish some degree of biochemical treatment.

Water Supplier: One who owns or operates a public water system.

Water Supply System: The collection, treatment, storage, and distribution of potable water from source to consumer.

Water Table: The level of groundwater.

Water Treatment Lagoon: An impound for liquid wastes designed to accomplish some degree of biochemical treatment.

Water Well: An excavation where the intended use is for location, acquisition, development, or artificial recharge of ground water.

Water-Soluble Packaging: Packaging that dissolves in water; used to reduce exposure risks to pesticide mixers and loaders.

Water-Source Heat Pump: Heat pump that uses wells or heat exchangers to transfer heat from water to the inside of a building. Most such units use ground water. (See: groundsource heat pump; heat pump.)

Waterborne Disease Outbreak: The significant occurence of acute illness associated with drinking water from a public water system that is deficient in treatment, as determined by appropriate local or state agencies.

Watershed: The land area that drains into a stream; the watershed for a major river may encompass a number of smaller watersheds that ultimately combine at a common point.

Watershed Approach: A coordinated framework for environmental management that focuses public and private efforts on the highest priority problems within hydrologically-defined geographic areas taking into consideration both ground and surface water flow.

Watershed Area: A topographic area within a line drawn connecting the highest points uphill of a drinking waterintake into which overland flow drains.

Weight of Scientific Evidence: Considerations in assessing the interpretation of published information about toxicity—quality of testing methods, size and power of study design, consistency of results across studies, and biological plausibility of exposure-response relationships and statistical associations.

Weir: 1. A wall or plate placed in an open channel to measure the flow of water. 2. A wall or obstruction used to control flow from settling tanks and clarifiers to ensure a uniform flow rate and avoid short-circuiting. (See: short-circuiting.)

Well: A bored, drilled, or driven shaft, or a dug hole whose depth is greater than the largest surface dimension and whose purpose is to reach underground water supplies or oil, or to store or bury fluids below ground.

Well Field: Area containing one or more wells that produce usable amounts of water or oil.

Well Injection: The subsurface emplacement of fluids into a well.

Well Monitoring: Measurement by on-site instruments or laboratory methods of well water quality.

Well Plug: A watertight, gastight seal installed in a bore hole or well to prevent movement of fluids.

Well Point: A hollow vertical tube, rod, or pipe terminating in a perforated pointed shoe and fitted with a fine-mesh screen.

Wellhead Protection Area: A protected surface and subsurface zone surrounding a well or well field supplying a public water system to keep contaminants from reaching the well water.

Wetlands: An area that is saturated by surface or ground water with vegetation adapted for life under those soil conditions, as swamps, bogs, fens, marshes, and estuaries.

Wettability: The relative degree to which a fluid will spread into or coat a solid surface in the presence of other immiscible fluids.

Wettable Powder: Dry formulation that must be mixed with water or other liquid before it is applied.

Wheeling: The transmission of electricity owned by one entity through the facilities owned by another (usually a utility).

Whole-Effluent-Toxicity Tests: Tests to determine the toxicity levels of the total effluent from a single source as opposed to a series of tests for individual contaminants.

Wildlife Refuge: An area designated for the protection of wild animals, within which hunting and fishing are either prohibited or strictly controlled.

Wire-to-Wire Efficiency: The efficiency of a pump and motor together.

Wood Packaging: Wood products such as pallets, crates, and barrels.

Wood Treatment Facility: An industrial facility that treats lumber and other wood products for outdoor use. The process employs chromated copper arsenate, which is regulated as a hazardous material.

Wood-Burning-Stove Pollution: Air pollution caused by emissions of particulate matter, carbon monoxide, total suspended particulates, and polycyclic organic matter from wood-burning stoves.

Working Level (WL): A unit of measure for documenting exposure to radon decay products, the so called "daughters." One working level is equal to approximately 200 picocuries per liter.

Working Level Month (WLM): A unit of measure used to determine cumulative exposure to radon.

X

Xenobiota: Any biotum displaced from its normal habitat; a chemical foreign to a biological system.

Y

Yard Waste: The part of solid waste composed of grass clippings, leaves, twigs, branches, and other garden refuse.

Yellow-Boy: Iron oxide flocculant (clumps of solids in waste or water); usually observed as orange yellow deposits in surface streams with excess iron content. (See: floc, flocculation.)

Yield: The quantity of water (expressed as a rate of flow or total quantity per year) that can be collected for a given use from surface or groundwater sources.

Z

Zero Air: Atmospheric air purified to contain less than 0.1 ppm total hydrocarbons.

Zooplankton: Small (often microscopic) free-floating aquatic plants or animals.

Zone of Saturation: The layer beneath the surface of the land containing openings that may fill with water.